Working with Emotional Health and the Enneagram

Working with Emotional Health and the Enneagram

Malcolm Lazenby
& Gayle Hardie

MONTEREY
PRESS

First Published in 2019
by Monterey Press
www.montereypress.com

Copyright © Malcolm Lazenby and Gayle Hardie, 2019

Author contact: leaders@globalleadershipfoundation.com
Website: www.globalleadershipfoundation.com

Cover artwork by Patrice Muthaymiles Mahoney.
Illustrations by Devon Bunce.

NATIONAL
LIBRARY
OF AUSTRALIA

A catalogue record for this
book is available from the
National Library of Australia

ISBN: 978-0-6481163-6-3

Thank you...

To YuPeng Qiu, who encouraged us to bring the work we do with our clients into something that everyone can read and use

To Devon Bunce, for her amazing ability to interpret what we do and bring it to life through the illustrations she has created

To Patrice Muthaymiles Mahoney, for her commitment to her country, her people, her practice and her love for humanity as she bought the gift of her art to our front cover, and

To David Brewster, who literally turned our knowledge and practice into the book you are holding.

Contents

Introduction

Building emotional health levels has always been at the heart of our work together. It was our intent for the Global Leadership Foundation when we established it in 2003: 'raising emotional health levels across the globe'.

We have been working with emotional health levels in business environments for nearly twenty years – across the private, public, not-for-profit and community sectors. Throughout, our main focus has been the development of leaders alongside transformational change in organisations. The application of emotional health to leadership was the topic of our first book, *The Emotionally Healthy Leader*, published in 2013.

Both of us also have long experience with the Enneagram as a model that can help individuals to understand their psychological patterns, including the triggers they react to and the underlying drivers of their actions.

The impact we have in our work is based on an approach that is focused first and foremost on the 'vertical development' framework of emotional health levels, with the Enneagram used as a tool for building self-understanding in those who work with us – self-understanding that is an essential component of moving up the emotional health levels.

We are continually looking to improve the effectiveness of our approach by learning from the experiences of both ourselves and others. Our approach in the use of emotional health levels and the Enneagram continues to be developed and refined as a result.

Our motivation for writing this book is three-fold.

First, we wanted to introduce the Enneagram in the context of the role it can play in moving up the emotional health levels. In sharing what we have learnt we combine an understanding of various Enneagram elements through the lens of emotional health levels and thus bring some clarity to areas of practice of the Enneagram not previously published.

Second – and in response to requests from many of our peers over the years – we wanted to share our knowledge and practical experience of how to move up the emotional health levels with a broader audience, as it is relevant to all of us.

Finally, we wanted to provide a practical set of self-development tools. Our hope is that any reader of this book, regardless of their prior exposure to this material, will be able to take the information, and in particular the development guides in Part 3, and start down the path of self-improvement.

Part 1 of the book introduces the key concepts we use in our work, including our model of the emotional health levels. This provides a platform for what follows. Part 2 is focused on the Enneagram and its relationship to our emotional health levels model, helping you to gain some insight into your primary Enneagram type and your current emotional health level. And Part 3 provides a substantial development guide, in which you can take what you've learnt about yourself from the first two parts and commence your journey towards moving up the emotional health levels.

Malcolm and Gayle

Part 1:
Understanding
emotional health

EMOTIONAL HEALTH IS a concept that is simple on one level and complex on another. It is simple in that once you understand its core principles, you will readily be able to apply those principles to the way you see and, importantly, engage with the world around you. However, emotional health is also complex in that it has many layers and there is always something more to learn. In this sense, gaining a full understanding of emotional health is an endless (but very enjoyable) journey, even for those of us who have worked with it for a long time.

You might already have come across the concept of 'emotional intelligence' (sometimes referred to as 'EI' or 'EQ'). Emotional intelligence is all about recognising and managing emotions in ourselves and others. It is a critical and interrelated 'subset' of emotional health, along with mental intelligence and other lesser known 'intelligences': body intelligence, heart intelligence, social intelligence and spiritual intelligence.

Emotional health 'wraps around' all these concepts, delving deeper into the ways in which each of us relates to, engages with and affects others and the world around us. It is a state of enhanced wellbeing created through highly conscious choices and mindful practices.

Vertical and horizontal development

Most of us have had the experience of attending a personal or leadership development workshop and coming away inspired. The best events leave our head spinning with possibility as we return home with a notebook crammed with good ideas for dealing with conflict, making meetings more effective or better managing our time.

Unfortunately, most of those ideas usually stay right where they are: in that notebook. We get back into our 'normal' life and world of work and before we know it the workshop and the inspiration it left us with have faded from view.

The problem is that many personal development and leadership development workshops simply focus on the delivery of knowledge and skills such as conflict management, facilitating effective meetings or managing priorities. While these are still very valuable, they are not enough on their own.

Fundamentally, skills-based training – which is also called 'horizontal' development – often doesn't take the personal side into

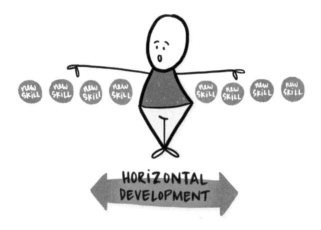

Figure 1: Horizontal development

account. It assumes the people engaging in the learning have the capability and mindset, and the right environment, in which to implement those skills. And it often fails to consider that the person doing the learning does not operate in isolation: that they will need to involve others in any changes they want to make, that those changes will affect others, and that those changes will also be affected by other change occurring around them.

Vertical development

While horizontal development is definitely necessary, in recent years there has been growing awareness and appreciation of the need for 'vertical' development as well.

Vertical development focuses on the individual as a person,

along with that person's interactions with others. It's about building our ability to comprehend and let go of limits on our thinking and perceptions, and in doing so more genuinely relate to and engage with others and the wider world around us. In short, it's about building self-awareness and the ability to work with that new-found awareness to become a better, more effective person.

We all have views and defence mechanisms about people and situations that keep us stuck in our current ways, as they feel safe and comfortable. When we let go of these fears and anxieties, our view of the world changes and we can change the course of how we think and feel and what we do.

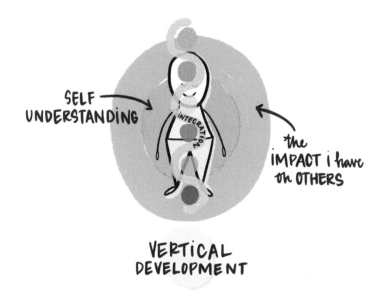

Figure 2: Vertical development

Vertical development lies at the heart of building emotional health, and therefore is central to this book, which is not about teaching you a set of new skills but rather helping you to better understand and appreciate yourself and the impact you have on others.

Above and below the line

There are two important frameworks that we need to introduce before we define emotional health and emotional health levels. The first framework is known as 'above and below the line' and relates to the responses we make to situations we find ourselves in and whether we are consciously choosing those responses or not.

Imagine you are in the car, driving along happily, when from out of nowhere someone cuts dangerously in front of you. You are forced to brake quickly to avoid an accident. What would you do next? If you are like most people you would probably react in one of the traditional ways: a heavy hand on the horn, a tirade of abuse, the flashing of headlights, or all three of the above.

This typical reaction to a common situation is a classic example of what we call an 'automated response'. It's 'default' behaviour: we don't consciously think about honking, swearing or flashing headlights – we just do it. Such a reaction is generally defensive and irrational, often full of blame, defensiveness, denying and justifying. However, we're not thinking about any of that at the time.

Now think about how, at some time in the past, you've

approached a conversation about your performance with a manager you didn't get along with. Did you go into the conversation with an open mind or were you on the defensive from the start? Did you find you were defending yourself early in the discussion, regardless of what the manager said? Most of us have been in a similar situation at some stage. Once again, it may only be later (if at all) that you realise that your responses weren't very open.

What is happening in this situation is very similar to what is happening in the road-rage scenario. The difference in the workplace is that instead of horn-honking, the automated response to being challenged or criticised is be defensive, to deny, to blame others or to justify.

In both these cases – the car and the workplace – there's a good chance that, on later reflection, you recognise that your behaviour was ultimately unnecessary and unhelpful and probably not the best choice you could have made at the time. But you may also wonder whether it is really possible to avoid these situations. After all, such responses are automatic, aren't they? Anyone would do the same in a similar situation, wouldn't they?

The truth is that it is possible to change your responses to both these situations, however doing so can require a substantial amount of work. The first step is to understand what is going on here.

In our work we draw a line – the 'line of choice' – between the default, automated responses to challenging situations (typically

Figure 3: The line of choice

denial, blame, justification or defensiveness) and the more emotionally healthy option of a thoughtful and constructive response to them (Figure 3). When we do the latter, we are taking *personal responsibility* – not for the situation itself but for the way we respond to the situation.

We say that automated reactions are 'below the line' while constructive, personally responsible responses are 'above the line'.

Notice that we use the word 'choice' here. For ultimately there is a personal choice to be made between operating above or below the line, even though it may not feel like it as our hand hits the horn or the excuses start flowing.

Making an above-the-line choice requires clear thinking and thoughtful, constructive responses. Achieving this in everyday situations takes training and practice, especially when you consider that making the choice has to be done very quickly. American psychotherapist and author Tara Bennett-Goleman calls it the 'magic quarter second': the time between when our brain absorbs a situation and our body reacts to it.

Some of that training and practice we get from life in general. As we 'grow up', we tend to learn to take more personal responsibility than we did when we were young. In practice, however, the vast majority of us only take personal responsibility for our behaviour and our responses some of the time, even as adults. At other times – when that other driver cuts us off, for instance – we slip below the line quite easily.

Spending some time below the line – defending, blaming, justifying – is quite normal for many of us. The challenge is to increase your awareness of these automated responses and, over time, to choose healthier ones more often. In other words, to constantly increase the frequency with which your response to challenging situations is 'above the line'. Achieving this will require a high level of awareness about yourself and the way you comprehend your interactions with others, which in turn requires another level of vertical development: getting to know your inner observer.

The inner observer

Imagine you are in a job interview. The interviewer asks you a question, which you answer. However, you know from experience that the interviewer is just as interested in the *way* you answer the question as in the answer itself. As a result, if you are conscious of this – if your 'inner observer' is active – you will:

- watch the interviewer for non-verbal cues and determine the impact of your response, as you are delivering it. For instance, are you getting a smile, a nod, a frown or a direct look? How positive do you feel as a result?

- be aware of your own body language and explore the impact these are having on you. How are you sitting – do you need to adjust your position? What about your eye contact and smile? What sensations are you noticing in your body – a dry throat, hot neck or chest, shaking hands or feet – and what might these mean for what you do next?

- use those non-verbal cues from the interviewer to remind yourself about what you could include if the next question is related to the one just asked.

Another way of understanding the inner observer is to use an analogy offered by Ron Heifetz in his book (with Marty Linsky), *Leadership on the Line*. Heifetz describes an imaginary dance floor overlooked by a balcony. He uses this image to advise leaders on

Figure 4: The inner observer

leading and navigating through change. In short, leaders need to be able to 'stand on the balcony' in order to get a 'big picture' view of what is going on, but at the same time they need to join the dance if they want to effect change.

It is the ability to do this – to be both 'in' the experience and outside it at the same time – that indicates your inner observer is working. This perspective enables you to see not only what is happening and what you are doing but also understand the impact you may be having on others.

Accessing the inner observer gives you the opportunity to make a conscious choice 'in the moment' of what you think is the best thing to do. When you do this, you will find yourself more constructive, calm, relaxed, connected and secure. You are also much more conscious of your current state of being.

It's very difficult to change your behaviours and the way you interact with others unless you're able to assess your existing behaviours and interactions in this way. People who are emotionally healthy are conscious of themselves – their thoughts, their emotions and their behaviours – and the impact they have on others. They are able to recognise and overcome the various influences and constraints they experience (either from others or themselves) through the choices they make and the practices they use.

They achieve this by being able to 'switch on' their inner observer. In the language of the line of choice, using your inner observer enables you to *choose* above-the-line responses to situations you find yourself in, as opposed to allowing automated responses to govern your behaviour. You are taking personal responsibility for your responses rather than reacting with denial, blame, justification or defensiveness.

Strengthening your inner observer comes with practice, through deliberately taking time before you respond to a situation and consciously making a choice about what you will do. The more you practise, the easier it becomes to be more aware of your emotions as things are unfolding around you, rather than after the event. You'll find that you can 'catch' yourself in the 'magic quarter second' referred to earlier. With increasing frequency, you'll be able to think before you act – to make a choice before you respond rather than responding automatically.

The acid test? When someone cuts you off in heavy traffic and instead of hitting the horn you are able to silently let the situation slide with no more than a wry grin. Once you can do this, you'll know that your inner observer is becoming more effective and that you are taking personal responsibility for your reactions to situations you find yourself in.

Building and strengthening your inner observer is a prerequisite for improving your ability to choose your responses and constantly appraising what you might do differently to have a more effective impact. Over time you will find yourself choosing better responses as well. And with that your emotional health will continue to improve, as we'll discuss much more.

Self-centredness

Earlier we distinguished between above- and below-the-line responses in terms of taking personal responsibility (above the line) as opposed to resorting to blame, defensiveness, denial and/or justifying (below the line).

Another way of looking at this distinction is in terms of 'self-centredness' or, more specifically, the 'degree of self-centredness' that a person has. This is the degree to which we are specifically focused on ourselves to ensure that we will survive in our environment. As such it also represents the degree to which we engage our defence mechanisms in an attempt to make sure we will feel safe.

A person with a high degree of self-centredness will tend towards blame, defensiveness, denial and justification in response to challenging situations. As they hit the car's horn they are instinctively blaming the other driver for cutting in front of them, taking their action as a personal affront. In contrast, a person with a low degree of self-centredness will be quick to consider the point of view and wellbeing of others as they go about their life. They tend to embrace the notion of the 'greater good'. They take personal responsibility for the impact they have on others, seeing themselves as one part of the wider community. If they hit the car's horn in an automatic reaction, their inner observer will soon have them experiencing some guilt at doing so. With a moment's thought they will choose to believe that the other driver probably had a reason for changing lanes quickly and recognise that they might have done the same thing in the same situation.

In our work we see self-centredness as a continuum. You're are not self-centred or otherwise. Rather, each of us has a degree of self-centredness and the more emotionally healthy we are, the less self-centred we become.

Behavioural freedom

As our self-centredness decreases, our degree of 'behavioural freedom' increases, and we are able to make more conscious choices around our behaviours in response to any given situation. This may seem like a fairly simple concept, but it is very important in understanding emotional health.

Earlier we mentioned the 'magic quarter second' as the time between when our brain absorbs a situation and when our body reacts to it. Someone with a high degree of behavioural freedom is well placed to use that quarter second to their advantage. Their inner observer will help them catch their automated response before it happens and instead choose how they will respond. They have the ability to choose an above-the-line response. In contrast, someone with a low degree of behavioural freedom doesn't have that control – that freedom to choose. They will react automatically and below the line.

With an increased range of behavioural freedom comes the ability to shift our concerns away from ourselves and towards others and broader social interests. In this sense, as we will see, a person's degree of behavioural freedom and their degree of self-centredness tend to be closely linked: as one goes up, the other goes down.

The centres of intelligence

The second framework important to an understanding of emotional health is what we call 'the centres of intelligence' or 'the three centres'.

If you were asked by someone to describe what you 'think' with, you'd probably look at them strangely and respond with 'My brain, of course'. Interestingly, it is not as simple as that. In fact, when we are thinking effectively, we are doing so not just with our brain but with our whole body.

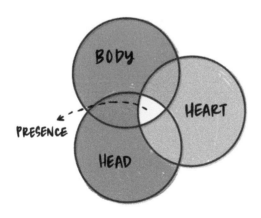

Figure 5: The three centres of intelligence

Three centres

Ancient eastern philosophy teaches us that clear, effective thinking is achieved using a balance of what we call the three 'centres of intelligence': the body or 'gut', heart and head (Figure 5). This notion is supported by modern neuroscience, such as in the work of Grant Soosalu and Marvin Oka and that of Antonio Dimasio.

Put very simply:

- When we engage the 'body centre', our 'body thinking' is based on what we sense and experience in the environment around us, that is our instinct – what we often call 'gut feel'. We also call this the 'doing centre'.

- When we engage the 'heart centre', our 'heart thinking' is based on what we are feeling through our connections with others, that is our intuition. We also call this the 'feeling centre'.

- When we engage the 'head centre', our 'head thinking' is based on objectively connecting our perceptions, knowledge and reasoning, that is our insight. We also call this the 'thinking centre'.

You might argue that instinct, intuition and insight are all pretty much the same, and in fact some dictionaries do list instinct and intuition as synonyms. However, we ask you to stay with us here. Looked at holistically, there is a subtlety to the difference

Figure 6: Body, heart and head

between the three centres that we feel is intrinsic in these words – a subtlety that will become clearer as we explore them.

We have found that providing examples assists in this clarification.

In the body centre we talk about instinct, which is where we get a 'gut feel' or a body sense of something we need to do. It is a sensation in our lower abdomen that we cannot ignore. We have many leaders who tell us that this is a primary input into their decision making and that it is never wrong. Recently we worked with a leader who went to great lengths to analyse a situation and the resulting decision he needed to make. However, no sooner had he made his decision than he knew it was the wrong one. His body centre – his gut feel – immediately told him he needed to do something else.

In the heart centre we talk about intuition, which is associated with feelings we get concerning people and relationships. This often occurs when a loved one tells us that everything is okay, though we can absolutely feel through our connection with them that everything is not okay. This feeling may prompt us to gently explore the situation a little more and, sure enough, we eventually learn that what our heart was telling us is right. We've heard many stories from people who tell us that they have had a sudden feeling of concern in their heart for a loved one who is somewhere else, only to find out later that, right at that moment, something unfortunate or concerning had happened to that person.

With respect to the head centre, reflect on a time when you faced a perplexing problem but, no matter how much you thought about it, you could not come up with an answer. Eventually you park the problem while you go about some other simple tasks (such as cleaning, gardening, washing dishes), and then all of a sudden the answer to your problem appears in your mind. This is insight. With practice we can increase the prevalence of this and also enable it to occur in the moment.

Various cultures use different language to express the concept of the 'mind' consisting of more than just the brain. It would be a good idea to explore your own experiences of the different types of thinking, in yourself and in others.

Each of us is capable of engaging all three centres: of thinking with our body, our heart and our head. However, in the process of developing a personality – which we'll discuss a lot more later in the context of the Enneagram – we tend to lean more strongly towards one of the three, which then becomes our primary filter for perceiving what we think is reality. We develop a tendency to trust the thoughts that come from our preferred centre over others. Conversely, we find ourselves mistrusting or avoiding what the other centres are telling us.

The thoughts and behaviours associated with each centre have different above- and below-the-line characteristics that in turn tend to be associated with high and low emotional health respectively. So, for instance, those who tend towards gut-thinking can be empowering and open with others in taking action when they act above the line, but they can be controlling and stubborn if they act below the line. Broadly speaking, people acting above the line in each centre look to adapt circumstances to meet their needs, whereas those acting below the line take a more defensive approach.

At first you may find it difficult to distinguish which centre of intelligence you most strongly associate with. However, as you learn more about the centres and practise distinguishing them in other people, you will notice the varying degrees to which you draw on instinct, intuition and insight – and one of these more often than the others – at different times. In truth you are probably already more familiar with this concept than you may be aware.

We will explain each centre in more detail in Part 2, in conjunction with the Enneagram types; as we will see, the centres of intelligence and Enneagram types have a close relationship.

Whole body thinking and 'presence'

While all of us tend to lean towards one of the three centres, the most effective thinking is achieved using the 'whole body', that is, by 'balancing' the centres. Whole body thinking is thinking that integrates the body, heart and head, regardless of an individual's bias towards one of these.

The most common times we think in this way are when we are at ease. Those times when we are sitting in the sun, walking through a forest or on a beach, playing with our children or literally 'smelling the roses'. It's thinking that, somewhat counterintuitively, doesn't feel like thinking at all. Sportspeople sometimes call this thinking being 'in the zone'. Others call it 'flow' or 'presence' (the term we tend to use).

In the information era, most people spend very little time being 'present'. Rather, our thoughts operate a bit like Twitter or Facebook: a never-ending stream of notes, recollections, to dos, ideas and inspirations. Time moves quickly as the mind shifts from one thought to the next. When operating in this way, as well as in times of pressure or stress, most of us will be skewed towards thinking and making decisions with our preferred centre.

As an example, imagine you are sitting in a meeting at work. An issue has come up in relation to a member of the team who has not completed his or her part of a task and the project you are all working on has stalled as a result. After a long conversation about the impact of this, everyone is starting to look to the leader, the most senior person in the room, to make a decision about what to do next. It is precisely in this sort of pressured environment that we tend to revert to our preferred thinking centre, so in this instance the leader is likely to draw on their preferred centre first. They will think and act, broadly, in one of three ways (before considering anything else).

The leader will probably either rely on 'gut' feel – on instinct – to make a call to action, paying less attention to the facts and feelings of those in the room or those who will be directly affected by the situation. Or they will rely on their heart – on intuition – to

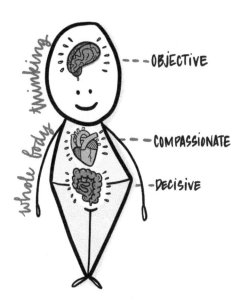

Figure 7: Whole body thinking

decide, doing the best they can to weigh up the emotional impact on everyone involved. Or they will rely on their head – on insight – to make a decision using reason and the objective data available to achieve a logical outcome.

It should be clear that each of these scenarios represents a quite distinct perspective on the situation and the way in which different people may respond.

If, however, the leader has a high level of emotional health, their response might reflect what we have been describing as whole body thinking, that is, the leader's thinking will draw on all three centres as guides to their response to the situation. Their response will be simultaneously decisive and compassionate, with perception and foresight.

In reality few of us will reach a point in which we perfectly balance the centres, especially when under pressure. True whole body thinking is something to aspire to. However, leaders with above-average emotional health will usually be more balanced, not simply relying on one centre to drive their thinking. They will be able to draw on the inner observer we described earlier and so access at least one of their less preferred centres. Again, we'll explore this concept further in the remainder of this book.

Emotional health

Having explained the various concepts central to understanding emotional health, including the above- and below-the-line and centres of intelligence frameworks, we're in a good position to properly introduce the concept of emotional health.

Emotional health is a state of enhanced wellbeing, characterised by a person's ability to be mindful and make constructive and respectful decisions and choices in every situation they find themselves in – that is, their ability to act (and respond) above the line. A person with a high level of emotional health takes personal responsibility for the way in which they relate to and engage with others and the world around them. Emotionally healthy people have a well-tuned inner observer: they are conscious of themselves – their thoughts, their emotions and their behaviours – and the impact they have on others. They are able to recognise and overcome the various influences and constraints they experience (either from others or themselves) through the choices they make and the practices they use.

In contrast, a person with a low level of emotional health will display self-centred, below-the-line reactions to situations they encounter, and they are less likely to be capable of responding in any other way (they have a low degree of behavioural freedom). Further, they are generally unaware of their reactions, so they remain oblivious to, for instance, the emotional pain they have caused someone through what they have done.

In terms of the centres of intelligence, a person with high emotional health is able to integrate the three centres and achieve whole body thinking more often than someone with average emotional health. A person with low emotional health will not experience whole body thinking at all and will, rather, tend to think from only their preferred centre. This is where we see a link between whole body thinking and behavioural freedom. When a person's three centres are well integrated, their range of behavioural freedom is higher. This enables them to be empowering, inclusive, idealistic, deeply caring, achieving, creative, wise, considered and visionary.

What increasing emotional health looks like

As people increase their emotional health they are better able to see other perspectives of the world they live in; they start to understand the assumptions that their own world view is built on and comprehend how others might form a different world view.

As they do this, they better appreciate that the coping strategies and defence mechanisms they have been relying on (likely characterised by below-the-line reactions, especially to stressful situations) have not served them well and in fact have held back their personal growth. In turn, those who increase their emotional health build increased resilience – physical, emotional and mental. Their approach to the way in which they engage, lead and relate with others, their communities and their organisations is constructive, generous and open.

With increasing emotional health, a person's 'inner observer' is activated more often. They frequently reflect on and appraise their own behaviours and responses. They identify areas of behaviour that could be improved and consciously plan to make these improvements.

Emotional health levels

The scale of emotional health levels

So far we've talked in general terms about the differences between a person who has a high level of emotional health and another person who has a low level of emotional health.

Of course, as with most things when it comes to humans, it is not that simple. We have developed a model for emotional health adapted from pioneering work by Don Riso and Russ Hudson and what they call the 'nine levels of development'. Our model identifies nine levels of emotional health, ranging from the highest level of 'presence' to the lowest level of 'delusional'. The model is shown in Figure 8.

In this model, we illustrate how degrees of self-centredness and behavioural freedom correlate with a person's level of emotional health. Put simply, the less self-centred someone is, and the greater their behavioural freedom, the higher their emotional health.

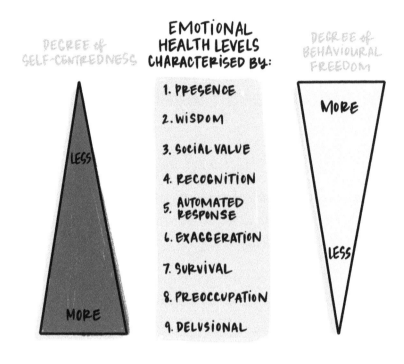

Figure 8: Emotional health levels

From the perspective of the above- and below-the-line framework, those with a higher level of emotional health will exhibit above-the-line responses to situations more often. Someone at emotional health level 3 will only occasionally go below the line, internally, and when they do so their inner observer will usually be quick to recognise this, causing them to adjust their response to the situation. They will almost certainly be regretful for any harm or discomfort they have caused another person. In contrast, those with a lower level of emotional health will display below-the-line reactions more frequently. We sometimes show the line of choice sitting between levels four and five.

At level 5 and below, the degrees of self-centredness and behavioural freedom are such that below-the-line reactions predominate – hence the label of this level: 'automated response'.

People with an emotional health level of 4 will display more above-the-line responses than below-the-line reactions and are generally aware of the impact they have on others. However, at this level there is still a tendency to hold strong personal preferences that influence the range of behavioural freedom available, an example of which would be choosing to meet individually with team members rather than as a whole group.

We can also look at emotional health levels from the perspective of the centres of intelligence. Those with higher levels of emotional health (level 3 or above) are able to draw on all three centres of intelligence and achieve 'whole body thinking'.

At average emotional health levels – between levels 4 and 6 – we have lost connection with one of the centres. We call this circumstance an 'imbalance of the centres', a concept that we'll explore in more detail later in the book when we look at development paths. Suffice to say for now that this imbalance of the centres means that true presence becomes elusive, as we are no longer capable of whole body thinking.

If we are unfortunate enough to fall lower in the emotional health levels – between levels 7 and 9 – we lose connection to another centre, leaving only our preferred centre as the one we can trust and operate from.

The levels in practice

A person with the highest level of emotional health – level 1 – is very rare. Such a person is entirely present with their environment and fully conscious of the impact they are having on that environment and the people in it. They are completely open, well balanced and liberated from any degree of self-centredness. Such a person is fully capable of choosing their response to any situation, and that response will always be above the line; they take personal responsibility for all their actions. People at this level define the term 'presence'.

In contrast, a person at level 9 has the lowest level of emotional health. They are entirely focused on their own needs, as that is the only way they know how to survive in their environment. They have little or no behavioural freedom to choose their responses to situations, and their responses will always be below the line: blaming, self-justifying, denying. People at this level almost certainly have a serious mental illness and are generally under medical and/or psychiatric care.

The vast majority of us sit somewhere between these two extremes, with most people around level 4, 5 or 6.

It is important to know that whatever level we are, we are not 'locked into' that level. On this we would make three points.

First, we all have good days and not-so-good days, and it's quite reasonable that on the former we might operate at a higher emotional health level than on the latter. For example, a highly emotional event can trigger a normally level 4 or 5 person to drop down to level 6, with their internal fears and anxieties manifesting in exaggerated behaviour such as angry outbursts, completely withdrawing or seeking out pleasurable experiences to avoid the pain. Fortunately, this will only be a 'spike' for most people and they will soon bounce back. On the other side it is also possible for this same person to spike to level 3 when, for instance, they find themselves fully engaged and connected with organisations and activities that embrace the 'greater good' and thus put aside their personal needs.

Second, we can improve our emotional health level over time – which of course is exactly what this book aims to demonstrate. For most of us, it would be our goal to do this.

Finally, none of what we are describing here is absolute. In practice, different people at the same emotional health level will have different responses and reactions, depending on their individual makeup or personality. There are also no hard, delineating lines between one level and the next. What we know is that some people have more emotional health than others, and the levels model is a good way of illustrating the continuum of emotional health between the two extremes.

What it means to be 'at a level'

It's easier to define what it means to be at a level if we describe in more detail some of the characteristics we would expect to see in people operating at that level. The way we like to explain this in terms of our model is to start in the middle and then describe the differences we see as we move up and down from there. Later we'll provide a little detail on the individual levels.

Summary of the nine levels of emotional health

For the purposes of this book it is sufficient to describe levels 3 to 6 in some detail, given this is the range in which the vast majority of people in the general population would find themselves and/or aspire to be. However, in order to complete the picture, below is a summary of each of the nine levels.

We want to reiterate the point that the levels are not absolutes: that we can fluctuate between one level and another for various reasons, including simply having 'good days' and 'not-so-good days', and that it is possible to improve our emotional health and move up the levels.

Level 1 – Presence

At this level a person has a quiet mind and is fully in touch with the present moment or the 'now'. Presence or 'flow' is the norm. They *are* happiness. They have total behavioural freedom and operate with complete integration of the centres of intelligence. Their inner observer is very powerful and they are present in all they do; each moment they are in is the most important and they are fully available to it. People who are able to attain this level of emotional health are extremely rare.

Level 2 – Wisdom

At this level a person has long periods of being present. With a very high degree of behavioural freedom and almost no self-centredness, they are able to integrate their experience, knowledge and life learnings and lead by example in ways that inspire and motivate others. They have a powerful inner observer and only very rarely allow an automatic pattern to dictate their behaviour. Nevertheless, there are still moments in their lives when they experience a 'default' response rather than making a conscious choice.

Level 3 – Social value

At this level, a person has a high degree of balance in their life and, for the most part, redirects their concerns to those of others and to broader social interests. A person who reaches this level has reduced their self-centredness by developing a willingness and desire to embrace the 'greater good' for their community/communities. With a high degree of behavioural freedom, an effective inner observer and the capacity for whole body thinking, they increase the number of opportunities to be 'present' for themselves and those around them. Their inner observer is used to monitor their own consciousness and behaviour and to bring them 'back into line' when they find themselves internally moving below the line in an automated response to some stressful situation.

Level 4 – Recognition

A person moving to this level from level 5 starts to recognise that they have choices with all of their reactions and behaviours and begins to observe them on a more regular basis. This observation helps them to increase their level of consciousness, which in turn leads to a greater degree of behavioural freedom. They also start to better integrate the head, heart and body centres and so increasingly create moments of 'presence' under certain circumstances. While a person at level 4 can still display automated patterns of behaviour, such responses are less likely to have a negative impact on others.

Level 5 – Automated response

At this level, roughly the level of the Western population on average, a person is dominated by a range of automated responses to situations they find themselves in. These automated responses are mostly defensive and reactive and are about controlling the environment (which can include the people in it) in order to get their perceived needs met. With a limited inner observer and a tendency to integrate no more than two of the centres of intelligence, their freedom to catch the 'magic quarter second' and react with greater personal responsibility is limited. Nevertheless, typically when the pressure is off, a person at this level is capable of making decisions and displaying automated responses that are less self-centred.

Level 6 – Exaggeration

At this level a person is more 'demonstrative' in their defences than a person at level 5. Their reactions are exaggerated as they over-compensate due to internal fears and anxieties. Their thinking takes place largely from the perspective of their preferred centre of intelligence, with limited connection to the other two. With a fairly ineffective inner observer they lack the capacity to reflect on their behaviours and therefore change them. As with level 5, though less often, the person at level 6 is capable, when circumstances allow, of making some choices in their reactions.

Level 7 – Survival

At this level a person's fears and anxieties become intolerable, as they believe there is little to support them in their life. They continually react to situations, they think only with their preferred centre, their inner observer barely exists and they have little to no behavioural freedom. Survival tactics become the focus of their world, giving them little or no control over making any reasonable choices.

Level 8 – Preoccupation

At this level a person starts to lose touch with reality, and their thinking, feeling, perceiving and behaviours all become severely distorted. They are out of control. This is considered to be a full pathological state and most people at level 8 or 9 would be subject to some form of medical care.

Level 9 – Delusional

At this level a person is delusional, out of touch with reality and willing to destroy others and themselves. This includes states of extreme psychosis, where they are totally uncontrollable and unreasonable. Their mind obsessions take over their life completely.

Leadership and emotional health

While the concept of emotional health levels can be applied to any individual, it gains even greater potency when it is applied to a leader. Of course, we are all leaders in some aspect of our life.

By definition, an emotionally healthy leader needs to display a minimum degree of self-centredness (after all, it's about others and the organisation, not themselves) and maximum degree of behavioural freedom (in order to make considered decisions rather than automatic or 'knee-jerk' ones). Leaders are expected to be both compassionate and caring as well as decisive and strong; doing this requires a high level of emotional health.

We find that leaders with an emotional health level of 4 or higher drive positive emotions in their workplaces. They create resonance by inspiring others through the creation of a genuinely shared vision, then coaching them to be all that they can be as they work towards achieving that vision.

We explored the relationship between leadership and emotional health in some detail in our first book, *The Emotional Healthy Leader*, published in 2013.

Part 2:
The Enneagram and
emotional health

THERE ARE MANY tools for discovering more about who you are, what you prefer and how you engage with others and the world around you. One of those, and the one we use in our work, is called the Enneagram.

Introduction to the Enneagram

We first came across the Enneagram in the late 1990s, some time before we started working together. When we settled on self-realisation as one of the three guiding principles for Global Leadership Foundation, it made perfect sense that the Enneagram would be something we could use. Since then, we have been fortunate to meet and work with many of the Enneagram's most prominent modern exponents, including Russ Hudson and the late Don Riso, Ginger Lapid-Bogda, the late David Daniels, Jerry Wagner, Andrea Isaacs, Uranio Paes, Peter O'Hanrahan and Tom Condon. As with emotional health, the Enneagram provides a source of endless learning.

The Enneagram is a powerful tool for personal development and transformation. It is especially useful in helping individuals to understand and improve their emotional health.

Stemming from the Greek words *ennea* (nine) and *grammos* (a written symbol), the nine-pointed Enneagram symbol represents nine distinct strategies – called 'types' – people use for relating to the self, others and the world. Each Enneagram type represents a different pattern of thinking, feeling and acting that arises from a deeper inner motivation or worldview. Each of the nine types has a 'gift' that it brings to the world.

Below (Figure 9) is the Enneagram symbol which shows nine points around a circle, each of which represents an Enneagram type. The internal lines represent a set of internal dynamics that we will explain later.

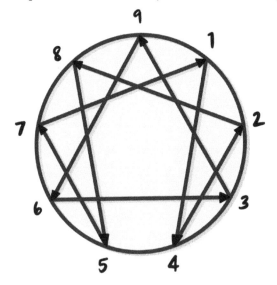

Figure 9: The Enneagram

At first glance the Enneagram may seem to be a personality profiling tool, akin to the Myers-Briggs profile, DISC or any of numerous other such tools. And while it is true that, as with those tools, undertaking an Enneagram type test will provide you with an indication of your 'type', this is just the starting point on a journey of self-discovery.

However, the Enneagram is also about wholeness in the sense that we are not necessarily restricted to a single type. When a person is at emotional health level 1, their complete behavioural freedom gives them access to the gifts of all nine Enneagram types.

For the vast majority of people, whose emotional health level sits between level 4 and level 6, there will be one type that tends to be more dominant in their thinking, feeling and behaviours. We refer to this as our *primary* type. Nevertheless, these people will still have a number of other Enneagram types that are strong for them, and they likely recognise at least something of themselves in all of the nine types. It is a *mix* of different types that tends to more strongly characterise who we are, even if one of those types is more dominant. We believe that each person is born with a primary type and that they then learn elements of one, or sometimes two, other types due to the influence of their primary care givers during those formative years up to seven years of age. In adulthood we often have another strong type, learnt from a career or other influence. Understanding this provides a growth opportunity. It allows us to understand how we can expand our behavioural freedom and embrace those other types as part of who we are. This often means overcoming the blocks that prevent us from behaving in certain ways.

Unfortunately, those who fall to level 9 on the emotional health levels (remember not to confuse the nine levels of emotional health with the nine Enneagram types) will contract into their primary type.

In exploring the Enneagram and learning about our primary type, we learn more about ourselves, about the gifts and limitations of that type, and about the likely nature of our relationships with others. None of these are absolutes – they are indicators at best – but they provide us with information and insights that we can then use to develop ourselves and increase our emotional health. However, the wholeness of the Enneagram provides the opportunity for all of us to move beyond our primary type to understand and appreciate each of the nine types as they pertain to both ourselves and others. Learning about the other types and their resulting gifts, as well as what occurs when they are over or under used, not only provides greater clarity around your own personality and preferences but it can also enable you to better understand others and why they do what they do.

The Enneagram and the centres of intelligence

The Enneagram is very holistic and correlates with the three centres of intelligence, which is one of the reasons why it has such close synergies with the exploration of emotional health levels.

As we have seen, achieving a balance of the centres of intelligence corresponds to a high level of emotional health. Our Enneagram type indicates a tendency towards one of the three centres (Figure 10). The lower our emotional health, the more rigidly we adhere to our type and its associated centre.

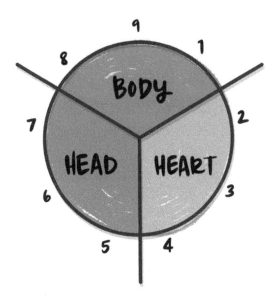

Figure 10: Enneagram types and the centres

To express this another way, having a high level of emotional health, and therefore a high degree of behavioural freedom and a balance of the three centres, gives a person 'access' to not only their primary Enneagram type, but to most or all of the other Enneagram types as well.

Even those with an average level of emotional health – those who often access only two of the three centres – tend to display characteristics of more than one Enneagram type, as we discussed above. It's our unique mix of access to the centres and strength in various Enneagram types that most strongly characterises who we are. Understanding our mix provides the opportunity for growth. For this reason, when we describe the Enneagram types in detail below, we will do so in the context of their associated centres of intelligence.

Emotional health continuums

Just as emotional health as a whole is represented by the continuums of self-centredness and behavioural freedom, so too can each Enneagram type be represented as an emotional health continuum. We will illustrate these continuums below, but suffice to say for now that each continuum represents the range of behaviours we would expect from someone of a given type who has a high level of emotional health (around level 2) down to someone with a very low level of emotional health (around level 7), along with the levels in between.

Gifts, fears and coping strategies

Earlier we mentioned the notion of the 'gift' that each Enneagram type brings to human nature as a whole.

People with high emotional health will mostly display above-the-line behaviours, and the specific way in which they do that is indicated by their primary Enneagram type. One person might tend to mentoring and empowering others while another will be achieving and engaging, and yet another will be considered and co-operative. These above-the-line traits are the *gifts* that each Enneagram type brings to the 'table of life'.

By contrast, each of us – especially and more frequently those with lower emotional health – is capable of displaying a below-the-line reaction to a given situation. Again, our Enneagram type indicates the specific behaviours we might enact. Where one person might be defiant and loudly uncooperative when challenged, another might be competitive and self-promoting, while yet another might be worried and pessimistic. The general term we apply to these behaviours is *coping strategies*. These are the mechanisms or behaviours we resort to when our degree of behavioural freedom is low, and they arise from the *basic fear* that is associated with each Enneagram type.

The psychology of this is that the gift of each Enneagram type is actually created from the associated basic fear and coping strategy for that type. A person's basic, underlying fear provides the underpinning motivation for the way they interact with the world – even if they have high emotional health.

At this point it's not important to understand this in any detail, but it will become more so as we start to work on your development path for growth later in this book.

Assessing your Enneagram type

Unlike some of the well-known profiling tools like DISC or Myers-Briggs, there is no single assessment questionnaire that will determine your primary Enneagram type. This is largely because of the 'wholeness' of the Enneagram that we described earlier – the fact that while we have one primary Enneagram type, we will also see aspects of ourselves in at least two or more other types. There is no single 'box' into which we can put ourselves.

Generally, our approach to using the Enneagram is to encourage the use of critical self-reflection, at least as a starting point. This can be done by reading through the descriptions of each of the three centres of intelligence and the nine Enneagram types offered below, while consciously noting aspects of yourself that you recognise in each. In particular, use the emotional health continuum offered for each type and mark off those characteristics that feel 'most like me'. It is likely that you will find one or two, perhaps three, types that stand out as candidates for your primary type.

Further self-reflection on reading through the additional perspectives on the Enneagram from page 103 will provide you with more evidence to help you build a picture of your Enneagram profile.

There are numerous online tools and smartphone apps available that, usually via a questionnaire, may be helpful in further 'narrowing the field' for you, or at least giving your more food for thought. However, bear in mind that none of these tools will provide an absolute answer. If, after exploring the process we have described above, you are still having difficulty identifying which Enneagram types are strong for you, or you simply want to assess your strong types more deeply, you may be interested in using the Enneagram cards that we have developed for this purpose. Information about these cards can be found at the back of this book.

The Enneagram types and their centres

What follows are brief descriptions of the nine Enneagram types. We recommend reading through each of the type descriptions, even if you think you have a good idea of which type or types apply to you. This will be helpful in the following sections as we bring the Enneagram and emotional health together and then discuss development paths.

For each type we describe a gift (the strength that this type brings to people of this type, those around them and their community), a basic fear (related to the primary need of their centre) and a coping strategy (the actions they take to avoid experiencing the basic fear). We also start to make links here between the Enneagram and emotional health.

When stepping through the Enneagram types, our approach is to work centre by centre, starting with the body centre. We therefore start with type 8, rather than type 1, and move around the circle from there. We will describe the 'body' types (8, 9 and 1) followed by the 'heart' types (2, 3 and 4) and finally the 'head' types (5, 6 and 7).

The 'body' centre: types 8, 9 and 1

Among the people you work with there will be some who are very aware of their immediate environment and instinctively sense what response is needed in any given situation. They move into action without requiring a lot of information or concerning themselves about the personal dynamics of the situation. In other words, they react first in an instinctual ('gut knowing') way. These are people who lean towards the 'body' centre.

The body centre is about gaining and maintaining autonomy and a sense of wholeness of oneself. It is concerned with making things happen, ensuring they are carried out in the right way and enabling others to be engaged and involved in achieving this. People who are strong in this centre have an affinity for 'living in the now'. They are generally more immediate, spontaneous and action oriented. They are conscious of resistance and control in their environments and maintain autonomy by being aware of what is happening and stepping up when needed.

Words that describe above-the-line behaviours associated with this centre include: accepting, mentoring, empowering, inclusive, resolute, congruent, harmonious, idealistic, aligned, impartial and discerning.

Below-the-line behaviours associated with this centre still focus on the maintenance of autonomy, but in a stronger, more self-centred way. It is about maintaining a sense of separateness and control. There is a deep underlying feeling of anger that comes when a person acting below the line senses they are losing their autonomy and this can manifest in taking rigid positions against the way things are. Their underlying feeling of anger or rage surfaces and is demonstrated in one of three ways (depending on their Enneagram type): they react to it, move away from it or try to control it.

Empowering, inclusivity and idealism become controlling, avoiding and perfectionistic.

Type 8: Empowering to controlling

Eights are powerful people. Concentrating on their own abilities to make things happen, they are blunt, firm, full of life, strength, and energy that they splash spontaneously in all directions. They like being thought of as determined and original people who could never unthinkingly follow the crowd or live a life of apathy. Some are loud and raucous, others are reserved and proper, but all are direct in communication. Justice is their issue, first for themselves and then for others. Having clearly defined ideas regarding what is just makes them extremely aware of how others use people and situations for self-serving reasons.

> *Gift:* The gift of Eights is the ability to bring genuine human strength and courage when facing whatever needs to be confronted. People with this gift are resourceful, decisive and self-reliant, dealing with difficult situations cleverly and effectively, without giving up or backing down.

Basic fear: Being harmed or controlled by others and thus becoming vulnerable.

Coping strategy: Exerting their will in order to remain strong and in charge of their life and that of others.

Eights are enabling, empowering and protective, using their strength to protect others from harm. They encourage others to be strong, confident and independent, empowering them to step in and take charge of their own destiny and development. They deal with what is in front of them, make things happen and constructively overcome challenges. They are usually the ones who say what needs to be said – who 'tell it as it is'. They take the initiative and embark on new ventures with boldness. They meet any moment with confidence. They will pursue their cause with relentless persistence, and in the process become champions for all the underdogs who lack the power and strength that Eights possess.

Although Eights exude tremendous strength, they seldom feel as strong and secure as they appear. They have an underlying fear of being harmed or controlled by others, and if they perceive this is happening, they can take advantage of others to (re)gain power and control. They are typically unaware that they are doing this. They are generally emotionally insensitive to themselves and others because they don't necessarily understand sensitivity, mistaking it for weakness or indecisiveness and so respond with disdain, anger or disgust. They generally express love for others through their actions rather than by verbally expressing their feelings.

Easily bored by routine and possessing an overabundance of energy, Eights doggedly manoeuvre through obstacles until they reach positions of influence and power. They generally live with the illusion that life is about having influence and making things happen; thus they rarely let down their guard and are always planning the next several moves to get ahead. They typically feel that everything depends on them and that they need to light a fire under others to get them moving. For them, life is always going too slowly. They like involvement and being on the go. They love stimulation.

Unconcerned or at least undeterred by what other people think or say, Eights have no fear of expressing themselves. They are able to handle pressure and stress, and so operate well during crisis. Experience has taught them to trust their abilities to be quick, thorough and creative in any situation, even the unexpected. Their self-confidence has grown from the awareness of their own capability and is often interpreted by others as arrogance because it lacks sensitivity. They need to feel strong because they are held fast by an internal experience of weakness, which they struggle to overcome.

Type 8 and its emotional health continuum

Eights who have higher emotional health levels can demonstrate real allowing and open-heartedness. Like all Eights, they know that they have the great strength to meet whatever comes up, but the presence that comes from balancing the centres enables them to surrender their need for control. As a result, they are very good at making things happen while empowering others in the process; they are good at stepping back so that others can step forward. They feel fully alive and experience each moment with a sense of wonder and a real willingness to be affected by what is present.

As they move down the emotional health levels, Eights find themselves resorting to their coping strategy more often. Their defensive reactions become more autocratic, demanding and controlling. They can be combative, hostile and intimidating, pushing people to their limits and using force and fear tactics to make others do things. They have a strong need to control the way things go, to avoid being vulnerable.

Figure 11 details the continuum of type 8 personalities across the range of emotional health levels.

	Accepting	I find peace, strength and serenity when I let go and allow events to take their natural course
2	Mentor	I see the potential in others and enable their development and progression
	Empowering	I encourage and enable others to be strong, confident and independent
	Enterprising	I take the initiative, embark on new ventures with boldness and make things happen
3	Resolved	I have inner determination, strength and constructively overcome challenges
	Protective	I use my strength, authority and resources to shield others from harm
	Decisive	I make choices quickly and confidently and rarely second-guess myself
4	No-nonsense	I am practical, efficient, straightforward, matter of fact and don't tolerate irrelevancies
	Direct	I am clear and straightforward, saying it like it is
	Dominant	I am stronger than others and take control of situations and people around me
5	Blunt	I am to the point and just say how it is going to be without factoring in other's feelings
	Controlling	I like to be in charge, control the situation and others and direct the results
	Belligerent	I am combative, hostile and push people to their limits, spoiling for a fight
6	Defiant	I am openly oppositional and uncooperative and refuse to obey
	Intimidating	I have no problem using force and fear tactics to make others do what I think they should do
	Vengeful	I get back at those who have insulted, wronged, injured or hurt me
7	Dictatorial	I force my authority over others in a harsh and unfair way as a mandate to get things done
	Ruthless	I do what I see is necessary without mercy or compassion

Figure 11: Type 8 continuum – empowering to controlling

Type 9: Inclusive to avoiding

Nines are easygoing people who value peace so highly that they can hold their personal relationships at bay through the power of their silence. Simply refusing to argue, they will leave the room – either emotionally or physically or both – rather than enter into any confrontation. Others can think what they like, say what they think, feel what they want, and Nines will simply do what they please. If they give in to the pressure of the moment, they know they will resent it later.

> *Gift*: The gift of Nines is the ability to bring a sense of peace and harmony to all situations. They are patient and diplomatic, able to find common ground and solutions, see multiple perspectives and engage others in dialogue around these.

> *Basic fear*: Being lost or 'separated from oneself'.

> *Coping strategy*: Forgetting themselves and seeking belonging.

Nines are balanced and have an inner calm that creates peace and harmony around them. They 'go with the flow', have an optimistic outlook and are fully interested in each moment they experience. They are calm, live without undue worry or concern and are generally laid back. They protect and enhance their reputation whenever possible and are respected both professionally and socially. What others think of them is important, because they can think so little of themselves.

Surprisingly, Nines are power-oriented people, though they use power in a quiet way. Their affability can disguise a fierce independence whereby they privately cling to their own ideas with stubborn tenacity.

Nines resist inner work. With an easygoing mask and lighthearted humour, they stay away from any activity that requires an examination of their own feelings. Holding an undercurrent of past resentment and pain, they fear that internal development might force them to face issues and cause turmoil and tension that they won't have the strength to handle. They strive to feel peaceful because they feel caught in continual distress that they want to avoid at all costs. They blend in and stay calm or give into others' agendas simply to avoid conflict, allowing things to happen to them and around them.

Nines use their tremendous strength to preserve the status quo rather than to accomplish goals. They ward off outside opposition with passive power. They interpret their laziness in the personal realm as humble acceptance. After all, in time everything passes, so why get upset about things you cannot change? Nines live with the illusion that professionally and socially they can do whatever is required.

Nines have a profound connection to the earth, often feeling at home and unthreatened in nature. They find that time outdoors restores the grounding that slips away in the activities and pressures of everyday life. They are generally attracted to outdoor pursuits because these reconnect them to their roots and give them the peace they long for. They can look like two different people in their private and public lives. At home or in the world of personal feelings and needs they will usually take the easy way out while in the external world all their best qualities shine.

Type 9 and its emotional health continuum

Nines who have a higher level of emotional health are balanced and resolute in all aspects of their life and relationships. While they are confident and clear about their ideas and opinions, they equally value others' contributions and are naturally inclusive. They bring a strong sense of peace and harmony to any situation and make others feel comfortable and at ease. There is a dynamic engagement with life and a harmonised flow about their way of being. They know that their wholeness comes from being actively engaged in life. They understand the value of rest, renewal and corresponding action.

At lower levels of emotional health, Nines use passive-aggressive tactics to get what they want and entrench themselves in comforting routines. This allows them to keep their anxieties and the world at bay. They become actively resistant to change when others make suggestions or try to influence them. They can also refuse to accept and admit what is true in favour of their own version of reality.

Figure 12 illustrates the continuum of type 9 personalities across the range of emotional health levels.

2	Resolute	I am generous and relaxed with grounded strength and confidence
	Congruent	I am composed and balanced in all aspects of my life and relationships
	Harmonious	My inner calm and tranquil presence creates peace and tranquillity around me
3	Patient	I comfortably wait, am calm, reassuring and do not interfere
	Inclusive	I engage all stakeholders in decisions that affect them
	Mediating	I bring people together and act as facilitator in conflicts, finding common ground and solutions
4	Easy-going	I am calm, not easily affected by events and not hurried or pushed by myself or others
	Seeing all sides	I see multiple perspectives and engage others in dialogue
	Agreeable	I lower my expectations of life and myself and go along with others in order to avoid possible conflicts
5	Accommodating	I oblige and give in to others even if it's not what I really want
	Neutral	I don't support any one position, and I am not invested in a particular outcome.
	Procrastinating	I tend to put things off until tomorrow and I have no sense of urgency about anything
6	Avoid conflicts	I avoid getting involved in order to stay out of trouble and conflict
	Stubborn	I actively resist change when others make suggestions or try to influence me
	Passive	I have no interest in things, people, or even my own life
7	Ineffectual	I am unable to produce results
	Neglectful	I don't take care of matters which require attention
	Inconsequential	I see myself as unimportant, letting others treat me poorly and doing nothing about it

Figure 12: Type 9 continuum – inclusive to avoiding

Type 1: Idealistic to perfectionistic

Ones are active, energetic people who tend to be self-starters attracted to the role of pioneering reformer. They are often at the cutting edge of a movement to improve a situation in their personal or professional lives. They keep a tight rein on their emotions, attempting to attain the perfectly balanced response to each specific situation they encounter. Internally critical, they often report that a mental voice points out faults and mistakes in both themselves and others. They can be compulsive list makers and, while this applies primarily to themselves, it is certainly not unheard of for spouses, children or co-workers of a One to have a to-do list handed to them at the beginning of a day or, even more frustratingly, at the beginning of a weekend.

> *Gift*: The gift of Ones is the ability to see clearly what constitutes the good, the just, the right and the proper.
>
> *Basic fear*: Being bad, defective or wrong.
>
> *Coping strategy*: Seeing what is wrong and needing to correct it; perfectionism.

Ones are idealistic and aim to be an exemplar operating at the highest standards. They are champions for justice and good causes. They use their innate sense of what is right and wrong to move clearly into the 'right action', prioritising what's important and organising themselves accordingly.

Born of their basic fear of being defective or wrong, Ones always look for ways to be right and can feel an obsessive need to correct any wrong. Before attempting something new – anything from trimming a bush to entering a new career – they are apt to read up on the topic to be certain that they will do it right. They are motivated to set the standard, to show by example and to be beyond reproach. They suppress anger and impulses in order to remain in control and continually compare themselves to others in order to maintain their 'rightness'.

They can be perfectionistic and may struggle to delegate because they often believe they are the only ones who can do something correctly. Their belief is that if they do what's right and expected, they will be in control. At the same time, because other people are not doing their share, Ones feel left in the lurch, with more than their fair allotment of responsibilities.

Ones are two-speed people: stop and go. Mostly on the go, they feel guilty for freeloading if they take time for themselves. Because they struggle with a need to be important, they work hard to earn their place. Consequently, they work long hours but often at a slow and steady pace, in order to meet their own idealistic standards.

Ones live with the tension of on the one hand wanting time alone but on the other hand needing relationships with others to ease their gnawing feelings of unworthiness and the associated insecurity. They believe they are not acceptable as they are: they must be better, always better. Ironically, when Ones unfairly vent their anger at others, they are usually more angry with themselves for not being perfect.

Ones can exude social charm with a ready smile, well-groomed appearance and a slightly shy hint of their desire to be liked. They generally come across as independent, capable of handling life and inexpressive of their own needs.

Type 1 and its emotional health continuum

At higher emotional health levels, Ones possess a real alignment between what they truly believe and a strong respect for what others bring. They know they are intrinsically good and can be fully appreciative of life as they find it, acting from a place of compassion. They understand there is more than one right way and that perfection lies in the eyes of the beholder, which makes them flexible and relaxed. They are non-judgemental, embracing the opportunity to better understand others' perspectives.

At lower levels of emotional health, Ones can be more critical, resentful, angry and self-righteous. They become more rigid in their thinking about what's right or wrong and how things should be done. They believe there is only one right way to do things and can become impatient with others who don't agree or comply, feeling fully justified in their uncompromising stance.

Figure 13 illustrates the continuum of type 1 personalities across the range of emotional health levels.

	Aligned	I am transparent and live in integrity with my principles and values
2	Impartial	I value and respect all perspectives and thoughts
	Discerning	I bring great insight and can distinguish what is important for others in any given situation
	Conscientious	My conscience guides my thoughts, decisions and actions in every matter
3	Ethical	I am directed by an inner sense of what is right and fair for everyone
	Principled	I know what I stand for and my personal standards manifest in everything I do
	Idealistic	I have a high set of ideals that I strive to meet at all times
4	Orderly	I am highly structured and I organize and manage my environment to ensure that everything is in the right place
	Diligent	I steadily persevere in carrying out tasks and duties in the correct way
	Obligated	I am convinced that I must strive higher and improve everything, including myself, others and the environment
5	Self-controlled	I watch myself carefully to ensure I do what is deemed acceptable .
	Correcting	I notice all flaws and errors around me and feel obligated to correct them
	Opinionated	I obstinately hold my own opinions because they are right
6	Perfectionistic	I strive for standards that are nothing short of "perfect" and reject anything that does not meet this
	Resentful	I experience myself simmering and angry about all the things that are not right
	Self-righteous	I alone have the truth and believe my views are always right and am therefore justified in what I do
7	Rigid	I take an uncompromising stance and am almost impossible to sway or influence
	Self-punishing	I punish myself severely for my flaws and errors

Figure 13: Type 1 continuum – idealistic to perfectionistic

The 'heart' centre: types 2, 3 and 4

The 'heart' centre is about interpersonal relationships and maintaining a sense of personal identity and worth. This centre is concerned with tuning in to and supporting other people's needs, ensuring that the way in which things are done meets others' expectations, and being able to express one's feelings in order to be better understood.

People who are strong in this centre build respectful interpersonal relationships, as they have a natural affinity for relating to other people. They value attention and/or validation from others, this feedback being a necessary component for them to thrive. They genuinely feel a range of emotions in themselves and others and connect into what is important for themselves and others through their heart. Their strong desire to engage and relate with others in order to be appreciated and valued results in them being highly intuitive to others' needs and wants.

Words that describe above-the-line behaviours associated with this centre include: honouring, deeply caring, sensing, gracious, admirable, self-assured, genuine, unique and appreciating.

Below-the-line behaviours associated with this centre include becoming manipulative and smothering, being opportunistic at the expense of others or becoming totally self-absorbed or 'dramatic'. Underlying feelings of unworthiness can surface when the attention and validation sought from others is not forthcoming. Such people can feel unloved, rejected and/or not worthy of attention. In order to counteract this, they seek attention or validation from others in one of three ways: they either continually give in in order to receive, pursue success in order to be valued, or create a unique identity for themselves in order to stand out.

Type 2: Deeply caring to smothering

Twos have an enduring compassion, concern and sensitivity for all of humanity. They also have a deep comprehension of and connection to their own and others' feelings, needs and emotional states. They are encouraging and appreciative and are able to see good in others. Because they focus their relational sensitivity outward, they are known as caring, considerate, kind, gentle and helpful. Twos can have an amazing intuition for finding people who need their care and knowing what others need. It's in everything they do – they are continually considering how to make connections easier. While they may not be able to pinpoint or recognise the specific need a person might have, they have an intuitive knowledge that something is not right.

> *Gift*: The gift of Twos is the ability to deeply empathise with others and be genuinely unselfish and compassionate in serving others' needs.

> *Basic fear*: Being unloved and unwanted.

> *Coping strategy*: Focusing on others' needs, assuming they will get their own met through giving to and being wanted by others.

Two's gentle and sensitive personality draws others towards them, into a warm and safe environment. Those others then feel free to be open, honest and vulnerable, which gives the Twos an inner warmth. This warmth vanishes when a Two is alone. When they are alone, a vague sense of meaninglessness begins to rise up and take their energy; time alone ends up being spent thinking of others. Their inner emotional life can feel arid and dull. Because they don't like being alone, they will drop everything to go to someone else's assistance. It is imperative for Twos to become proficient at generously responding to the needs of other people. The gratitude and appreciation that usually results will tend to ease their constant internal loneliness.

Twos are often drawn to a helping profession where their desire to support others can be put to good use. However, in responding to others' needs they tend to simultaneously create deeper needs that only they can fill. They create dependency in other people because they are totally dependent on others for their personal sense of wellbeing and worth. In short, they are externally competent and internally dependent. On the surface Twos seem to be offering love, but on a deeper level they are really searching for it.

Twos extend themselves to others with affection, gifts, services and many other things but are often disappointed by the responses they receive. Blind to the dark side of their motivation, they narrowly focus on the results of their helping, allowing the warmth of their personalities to play a key role. They tend to resent a person who refuses their help or who attempts to establish a reciprocal relationship. Taking pride in their virtuous, self-sacrificial attitude towards life, they wonder why so few people are 'other centred' and conclude that most people simply are selfish.

By concentrating on the interpersonal realm so intensely, Twos allow their personal lives to become disorganised, responsibilities to be ignored and many personal projects to be left only partially completed or undone altogether.

Type 2 and its emotional health continuum

For Twos with a higher level of emotional health, their giving and generosity is genuine. They understand that their self-worth is not solely attached to others loving or liking them. They recognise that while strong relationships are important, they also need to take care of themselves in the process. Twos with high emotional health know that empathy isn't about sympathy but is rather about appreciating and supporting another person where they are. They are often recognised as natural coaches, given the way they engage and show their interest in and genuine concern for other people.

As they move down the emotional health levels, Twos can get manipulative. They can feel 'burnt out' and unappreciated because they believe they are doing so much giving but not receiving anything in return. Given that, they can become calculating in finding ways to get their needs met. They react by being wilful, thinking that they can make others love them. They can begin to create needs in others that make themselves indispensable, while their giving and generosity begins to have lots of strings attached.

Figure 14 illustrates the continuum of type 2 personalities across the range of emotional health levels.

Type 3: Achieving to opportunistic

Threes are smooth, 'political' people. They are critically attuned to the feelings and needs of others and use these perceptive capabilities to engage others in supporting any goal or project that could enhance their own self-image of confidence, competence and capability. These hardworking, assertive go-getters measure their success by the amount of praise they are given by other people. Threes have selective memory, recalling successes above failures. If their success depends on compromising personal values and standards, they easily find a reason for doing so. When faced with failure, they can walk away and never look back, their loyalties suddenly disappearing.

> *Gift*: The gift of Threes is the ability to bring energy, talent and organisation to make things happen and deliver results.

> *Basic fear*: Being worthless and having no value apart from one's achievements.

> *Coping strategy*: Accomplishing tasks and goals in the most efficient and expedient way to gain the attention of others.

	Honouring	My relationships reflect and respect both my own and others' wishes, hopes and dreams
2	Deeply caring	I hold deep compassion and love for myself and others
	Sensing	I have an intuitive awareness and deep comprehension of others' emotional states
	Nurturing	I genuinely care for the well-being of others and support them to be all that they can be
3	Generous	I share my resources abundantly to benefit others
	Serving others	I am unselfish in sustaining and dignifying the lives of others
	People pleasing	I like people to notice how much I care about and feel for them
4	Needing closeness	It's important to me that I am personally close and intimate with others
	Flattering	I compliment and admire others so that they like me
	Possessive	I can become pushy and smothering about staying close and needed by others
5	Intrusive	I interfere in areas where I am not welcome or wanted to make sure that I am important to others
	Self-sacrificing	I overextend myself, helping too many people and feel burdened as a result
	Prideful	I believe others need help and I don't
6	Self-important	I have too high an opinion of my own importance in helping others
	Martyring self	I go so far with service and generosity to others that my own needs are never met
	Manipulative	I am deviously skilful at making situations go my way in order to get the attention I desperately want
7	Co-dependent	I control everything in order to have others need me
	Self-deceptive	I fool myself by believing that others need me more than they do

Figure 14: Type 2 continuum – deeply caring to smothering

Threes have a talent for seeing the most efficient way to achieve a goal and earn the reward and recognition they expect (and need) as a result. They are motivated to be recognised and admired by others for their achievements and can be highly focused and goal driven, often putting their feelings aside to get the job done.

Things seem to come easily to Threes. They are self-assured, talented, gracious and authentic, with a spirited 'can-do' attitude towards life. They are able to read contexts well and work out how to be appropriate in different settings, adjusting themselves as needed to achieve the best outcome. They tend to think that everything will work out fine; if it doesn't, it probably wasn't any good to begin with.

Threes tend to relate personably, but not personally, to people and to life. Often they don't set boundaries between their personal and public lives. They are professionals on twenty-four-hour call, parents who use every opportunity to teach their children what they will need in daily life, people who identify so much with their role that they have difficulty just being themselves.

Threes often think that their external image is reality. Appearance – how they look, produce, perform – is the only thing that counts. However, underneath this self-assured exterior lies a volcano of emotion. They are passionate about life and have deep feelings about many things, but they are very cautious about revealing their thoughts or feelings to other people. In their personal relationships, they have learned that others are usually incapable of handling the intensity of their emotions, while in the work world they believe that any self-revelation would be political suicide. Thoughts, feelings and personal values are private and therefore insignificant. If you expose your private life, you will never get ahead nor convince anyone you are worth anything, so the only safe place to deal with emotions is in private. While this creates a tendency for loneliness, it is much easier to deal with that than the complicated messiness of intimacy.

Thus Threes live in two worlds simultaneously: one in the spotlight at centre stage and the other on a secret island of isolation where feelings hide behind masks, failures behind successes and vulnerability behind competency. Too shrewd to tell an outright lie, they simply won't reveal anything unless it will ultimately be to their advantage. Any doubt on this score and they take the prudent path of silence. Their vision can become so clouded that they are unable to distinguish between real life and play acting, truth and deception.

Type 3 and its emotional health continuum

At higher emotional health levels, Threes recognise that their personal value is not wholly attached to outcomes and that they are valued for who they are as a person as well as what they achieve. They engage others with ease and encouragement and are gracious in recognition, attributing success and outcomes to others as well as recognising the part they have played themselves. They are role models who embody the values affirmed by their cultures and communities. They are self-developing, always working to improve themselves, and they have the energy to be the best they can be. In addition, they are genuine, sincere, authentic and confident about who they are. They do not feel compelled to make adjustments to meet external standards or expectations.

At lower emotional health levels, Threes can get overly competitive and deceptive. Their tendency is to find quicker ways to achieve their goals, no matter the cost. It's not the journey, but the end result that is the focus. They have a tendency to move ahead of other people. When it comes to success or values, success is more important and they are willing to bend the rules to achieve it. Threes with low emotional health become more and more concerned about their image and making a favourable impression on others. They constantly brag about themselves to let others know how good they are, even exaggerating or lying about their contributions, achievements and possessions.

Figure 15 illustrates the continuum of type 3 personalities across the range of emotional health levels.

2	Gracious	I am warm, courteous, and kind; with an ease in the way I live my life
	Admirable	I am held in the highest regard for my realness, heartfelt sincerity and authenticity
	Self-assured	I truly feel that I am of value and comfortable with who I am
3	Engaging	I effortlessly communicate what I value in ways that inspires others and enables their understanding
	Role model	I embody widely admired qualities affirmed by the culture and my social environment
	Ambitious	I improve myself and develop my potential so that others will want to follow my example
4	Seeking recognition	I am motivated by being noticed, recognised and admired by others for my achievements
	Efficient	I am highly focused and goal driven, putting feelings aside to get the job done
	Image conscious	I am very concerned about my image and making a favourable impression on others
5	Competitive	I want to be the winner; therefore I have to do better than others in all areas of life
	Chameleon	I adjust my behaviour to suit the particular context so others will think well of me
	Expedient	I take easy methods or shortcuts to get things done
6	Self-promoting	I constantly talk and brag about myself to let others know how good I am
	Pretentious	I exaggerate my contributions, achievements, possessions and lifestyle
	Taking credit	I take the praise and attention from others for things I didn't do
7	Covering up	I hide the truth to maintain the image of success
	Deceptive	I lie and deceive to avoid owning up to my failures to make people believe something different than what is
	Opportunistic	I take advantage of people and situations to advance my own interests with no regard for principles or people

Figure 15: Type 3 continuum – achieving to opportunistic

Type 4: Creative to self-inhibiting

Fours have an uncanny ability to see things that other people don't see. They have a wonderful aesthetic sense and appreciation for beauty. They are creative, self-revealing, self-expressive and self-aware. They are completely in touch with and capable of expressing their feelings and thoughts and helping others to experience the same depth of expression. They have an ability to create meaning from personal experiences and willingly share these to build greater understanding. They have a spacious heart, demonstrating real equanimity with others and are accepting of the full range of emotions, expressing them deeply and freely and without attachment to or rejection of any of them.

Gift: The gift of Fours is the ability to appreciate the true beauty and uniqueness in people, things and the world around them.

Basic fear: Not having any identity or personal significance.

Coping strategy: Searching for the ideal – in love, in others and in the world around them.

Fours are centred in their emotional life, which they experience as an intense and private world that no one else understands. These are people who have deep feelings and who believe that strong passions are the essence of real living. Their personal sensitivity and a keen desire for intimacy lead to a need to be included and invited into groups, and to include others in their groups. They tend to experience emotional extremes that range from the light, bright and fantastic to the heavy tone of the low, dark and sombre. This exaggerated emphasis on feelings is given expression through their dramatic style of response and interaction.

Fours often feel the need to create something (through visual, creative or performing arts) to give expression to their feelings, because words are too mundane and beauty is so hard to describe in ordinary language. They like to dress differently, do special work and have unusual things, often feeling compelled to be mysterious and create an alluring aura to gain others' attention. Their home and their expression of their personal environment can be very important to them, providing a place where they feel secure and can be themselves in an atmosphere of both intimacy and respect.

Fours can be engulfed in insecurity when their feelings of inferiority collide with their intense need for intimate relationships. They fear they will be rejected for someone more interesting or appealing and will cling too tightly and become possessive. Their fear then becomes a self-fulfilling prophecy. The sense of loss and loneliness that follows causes them to re-create and mull over every moment, not just of that experience but of their entire history of disappointments with people. They analyse and reanalyse the past in an attempt to understand and resolve the pain they carry. They believe that to understand and be understood by even one person is the key that would open the door to real life.

Fours are hyper-aware of all the good qualities and possessions of others, while not seeing their own hidden strengths. They generally want what other people have. They live with the illusion that they can never really live life to the full until they have developed all their potential and thoroughly understood themselves.

By constantly comparing themselves to others and highlighting all they cannot and do not have, they allow their inner life to be dominated by an intense attitude of pessimism. This negative outlook leads them to look first at the obstacles and pitfalls in any project or life situation. If they always prepare for the worst, they protect themselves from unexpected disappointments.

Type 4 and its emotional health continuum

Fours with higher emotional health levels have an ability to see the unique and special qualities in both themselves and others. They can share how they are feeling and they help others to feel more deeply through creative and supportive approaches to expression.

At the other end of the scale, Fours with lower emotional health levels find that their uniqueness and specialness isn't there in the way they want it to be. They can feel tormented, experiencing a despair that comes from a feeling that they have no identity and therefore no worth. They become very internally focused and self-absorbed, some would say 'dramatic'. In this state they can be self-indulgent and self-pitying, waiting for someone to rescue them. In some instances they place so much attention on themselves that they believe they cannot be bound by ordinary rules or expectations and exempt themselves from living ordinary lives.

Figure 16 illustrates the continuum of type 4 personalities across the range of emotional health levels.

2	Genuine	I am true and deeply connected to my origins, my values and myself
	Unique	I bring a different, creative and characteristic perspective to all that is around me
	Appreciating	I experience an overwhelming feeling of wonder and admiration for the beauty in and around me
3	Self-revealing	I openly share what is personal and important to create greater understanding
	Artistic	My creativity and inspiration comes from a deep place within me and reflects my feelings and who I am
	Sensitive	I am acutely aware of what is going on around me and adjust how I am accordingly
4	Romantic	I am attracted to those who indulge me and pay attention to my special desires
	Aesthetic	I am attracted to beauty in people and things as it stimulates my feelings and reinforces my sense of self
	Special	I want others to recognise and appreciate the qualities that are unique to me
5	Brooding	I replay negative feelings from the past and return to them again and again
	Misunderstood	I feel inadequate as I believe others do not understand me at all
	Temperamental	I have moods that are unpredictable and insist others respect the delicacy of my feelings
6	Self-pitying	I feel sorry for myself and seek sympathy from others as a result
	Envious	I am preoccupied with and long for what I perceive others have and what is missing in my life
	Hypersensitive	I overreact, overanalyse and imagine others' responses (or lack of them) are all about me
7	Victimized	I feel helpless in all situations and my despair continues to reinforce my victimization
	Self-inhibiting	I am unable to engage in anything and am therefore totally ineffective in all of life's doings
	Apathetic	I am void of feeling and am indifferent to what is going on around me

Figure 16: Type 4 continuum – creative to self-inhibiting

The 'head' centre: types 5, 6 and 7

The third broad group of people you will find are those who prefer to use their thinking to interpret and appreciate a situation, then use that insight to work out what they believe will be needed. These 'head-centred' people seek security in the choices they make and using their insight helps them feel prepared to cope with what they anticipate might be ahead.

The head centre is about finding an inner sense of guidance and support. It involves understanding and synthesising information to increase knowledge and strengthen learning, exploring and understanding risks and consequences that impede progress, as well as remaining enthusiastic about and open to what is possible. People who are strong in this centre can be considered and reflective, use inner guidance to connect with what really is, are perceptive and curious about the possibilities that exist, and strategise for the future. They gain security through knowing and become known for their planning and problem-solving prowess.

Words associated with above-the-line behaviours in this centre include: perceptive, ingenious, curious, alert, self-reliant, mutually accountable, joyful, enthusiastic and versatile.

People strong in this centre shift below the line when they think their security is threatened. Their underlying feeling of fear surfaces and is enacted in one of three ways: they turn to an inner authoritative source looking for more and more information, they look to an approved or tested authority for validation and support, or they busily, even frantically, look for alternative pleasurable ways to move forward to avoid the fear. Wise, considered and visionary become isolated, self-defeating and scattered.

Type 5: Wise to isolated

Fives can observe the world and make sense of things. They have extraordinary perceptiveness and understanding. They are wise, independent, clear thinkers who can remember details and are not easily pulled in by conventional ways of looking at things. They are mentally alert, curious and have a searching intelligence: nothing escapes their notice. Fives develop a mature compassion in their heart, as they are able to stay with the feelings and emotions this brings without contracting away into the safety of their minds.

> *Gift*: The gift of Fives is the ability to understand meaning and connection and thereby achieve genuine insight and grounded wisdom.

> *Basic fear*: Being incompetent, useless and incapable.

> *Coping strategy*: Collecting and analysing information to build their knowledge and capability.

The strength of a Five lies in their ability to perceive and comprehend life on a broad scale. They quickly sift out feelings from facts then pierce through to the core of the issue to summarise life, people and situations with a dispassionate logic that's as often tactless as it is accurate. Because they are emotionally unattached, they excel at delegation, mediation, diplomacy and research. They also love adventures – vacations to interesting places, skulking in the nooks and crannies of 'out-of-the-way' destinations, discovering new paths to knowledge or understanding – for these are opportunities to learn and add to their personal library of little known, extraordinary information.

Fives feel deeply about much of life but generally don't show it. In their desire to be seen as capable and competent, they employ a coping strategy of collecting and analysing information to build their knowledge and capability. They focus on gathering, researching and observing until they can figure out where everything fits in the scheme of things. They intentionally isolate their feelings so they won't interfere with the logical evaluation of a person or situation. They tend to ignore relational and emotional issues when trying to solve problems, or in living life in general. They need time and space alone to think, ponder, and reflect. No matter how much they have learned about life, a Five never feels quite ready for or capable of taking on the responsibility of direct involvement or commitment.

Fives are reserved people who strive for an objective, dispassionate perspective. They can often come across as loners or detached people who resent intrusion. However, they often secretly feel lonely and hope that someone interesting who is involved in life will show up on their doorstep for a casual visit. They are unlikely to initiate such an invitation, as they dread the possible pain of rejection.

Fives are often witty, charming and attractive people who are the last to know they are likeable. Their non-conforming attitudes and unusual insights into life make them clever and interesting conversationalists. They love to perpetuate their unorthodox, slightly eccentric image and they sometimes use it to excuse themselves from developing social skills or becoming too involved in life. They feel inadequate as human beings and believe that a wealth of uncommon knowledge, time and original insights will make up for their deficiencies. They live with the illusion that knowing about life is the same as living it. They want to be known as wise, though their slightly superior manner can be intimidating or even irritating to others.

Type 5 and its emotional health continuum

Fives with a higher level of emotional health are confident in their own ability and are comfortable to step forward, whether they know everything or not. They are curious, willing to tinker and play and explore possibilities, inventive with a desire to create and synthesise ideas. They will engage in physical activity, quieten their minds and consciously not allow themselves to get distracted by more and more information, making genuine and direct connection with life around them.

As they move down the emotional health levels, Fives become even more immersed in their own mind and knowledge. They begin to disassociate and further push away from their feelings to concentrate more deeply on the facts. They become isolated and insensitive to emotions. Objectivity is still available, but it causes a compartmentalisation of feelings and facts in which feelings and emotions are put aside in order to protect themselves and to remain competent in their own eyes. Fives with low emotional health can also get into a speculating loop, continuously pondering possibilities and ideas, detached from people, events and feelings.

Figure 17 illustrates the continuum of type 5 personalities across the range of emotional health levels.

Type 6: Considered to self-defeating

Sixes are natural troubleshooters, seeing potential hazards, issues and problems that may affect both themselves and others in any situation and developing and offering timely and relevant solutions. When they can see a problem, resolve it and sort things out, they will then keep their 'eye on the flock', ensuring their safety and that they stay on course. Sixes develop and build loyalty and commitment from others as a result. They understand that when each and every person does their part for the team, everyone is better off. They take their place and do what is expected of them, trusting that others will do the same, thus ensuring that everyone is contributing to the greater whole.

2	Perceptive	I integrate the use of all my senses and provide great insight
	Ingenious	I delve deeply into what is available and evolve new and inventive ideas as a result
	Curious	I seek to know and understand more of what is beyond the usual and expected
3	Insightful	I provide considered responses and insights beyond just data and facts
	Inventive	I synthesize data and ideas to create and discover something new and better
	Exploratory	I curiously explore what else might be possible and consider new and different ideas and opinions
4	Objective	I understand and share what I know in an unbiased and unemotional way
	Analytical	I can break things down logically and systematically to make sense of things
	Specialising	I focus on a small number of areas to gain mastery and feel competent
5	Detached	I separate myself from people, events, and feelings in order not to be affected
	Speculating	I continuously think about and ponder on other possibilities and ideas
	Secretive	I am unwilling to talk about my personal life so that others do not have power over me
6	Disassociating	I push away and separate from my feelings to concentrate on the facts
	Subversive	I undermine others by indirect means using my knowledge as a way of unsettling them
	Provocative	I am eager to deflate conventional opinions and adopt views that are deliberately different to those of others
7	Isolated	I separate myself from others and have difficulty connecting
	Obstructing	I am in a state of constant opposition and devalue all opinions and ideas other than my own
	Nihilistic	I am sceptical about reality, knowledge and deny all established authority

Figure 17: Type 5 continuum – wise to isolated

Gift: The gift of Sixes is the ability to actively support and steadfastly commit to people, groups and causes, ensuring their ongoing safety and security.

Basic fear: Having no support and guidance.

Coping strategy: Vigilantly noticing potential hazards, preparing for worst possible outcomes and guarding against the dangers of the world (including people).

Sixes are information-oriented people who take their responsibilities very seriously. Caution permeates their personality and lifestyle. They will never jeopardise themselves or those they love through reckless action or careless thinking. Sixes dedicate themselves to upholding and passing on sound moral values, for they know these are the basic foundations of a strong, healthy society.

They have an underlying sense of insecurity and a desire to be included that often leads to an exaggerated need for reassurance and personal contact. They deal with their own insecurities by defining morality in a rigid way, and can then become opinionated and unforgiving of all who hold different values. To their way of thinking, fear is prudence – it motivates a need to gather the information required to make decisions. They live with the illusion that although life is dangerous, they can make it safe with thorough preparation and a responsible attitude.

The Six's path is one of duty and dedication. They can prefer to keep to tradition in such areas as relationships, beliefs and principles because they trust what has been proven to work and fear the risk involved in attempting anything new. Sixes are the most naturally domestic of all types and often become the information hub and the gathering point of the community they most value. When their primary group is the family – and often it is – good solid values will permeate everything from child rearing to family celebrations. If they commit themselves to another kind of community – a work organisation for example – the customs, norms and values of that community will provide the Sixes' foundation and values.

Sixes are always enquiring – either directly or indirectly – about what is going on in the lives of everyone they know. Keeping abreast of personal information about other people helps them feel connected and alleviates their fear of being left out or shunned. Remaining active eases their anxiety because it eliminates spare time in which worries and concerns might otherwise dominate their thoughts. Being accepted by social groups soothes their greatest worry – that there is nowhere they truly belong. Constant and tangible signs of reassurance give them a sense of confidence that they are doing well, that they are liked, and that they are welcome. Without this reassurance their anxiety can grow to a point where they become fearful about possible or imagined threats to their security.

On the lighter side, laughter and fun will be the highlight of the day or week for Sixes as a needed release from their energetic and hardworking daily routine. Graciousness will often permeate their everyday demeanour and will generally be their hallmark in social situations. However, if they are crossed, a backbone of steel – the origin of which is annoyance at not feeling accepted or respected – will make them stubborn, tough negotiators.

Type 6 and its emotional health continuum

At higher emotional health levels, Sixes are strong and clear in their convictions and thoughtful and engaged in what is required to move forward. They are self-affirming, trusting of self and others and are strong collaborators. They have a belief in themselves that leads to courage, positive thinking and staying the course, despite difficulties. Their fortitude and perseverance inspire loyalty in others.

At lower emotional health levels, Sixes are easily triggered, highly reactive and continually doubting. They have difficulty getting past their anxiety and begin to self-sabotage themselves because they fear they cannot do something, which then becomes a self-fulfilling prophecy. Even when opportunities present themselves, they may not accept the invitations placed in front of them because of their doubt and worry. As they become doubtful and untrusting of themselves or others, they get locked into a tight world ruled by a 'multiple committee' in their head. This back and forth thinking results in doubt, worry, anxiety and a lack of peace of mind.

Figure 18 illustrates the continuum of type 6 personalities across the range of emotional health levels.

2	**Alert**	I am responsive and perceptive, taking action so that everyone around me is safe
	Self-Reliant	I trust in my own ability to meet and deal with any challenges I face
	Mutually accountable	I ensure that mutual promises and commitments are met through working with and engaging others
3	**Persevering**	I stay on course despite difficulties, obstacles, or discouragement
	Trouble-shooter	I consider all angles and am ready for any potential problems
	Cooperative	I am willing to work together and share responsibilities for everyone's mutual benefit
4	**Dutiful**	I do what I am expected to do to fulfil my obligations
	Seeking reassurance	I look to others to validate that I am on the right path
	Cautious	I restrain myself from taking action without thorough consideration
5	**Worrying**	I overthink and get anxious about situations and problems
	Indecisive	I am unable to make my mind up about which is the best thing to do
	Doubting	I am sceptical and continually question things, which results in constant uncertainty
6	**Pessimistic**	I always expect the worst to happen
	Suspicious	I question the motives of others and tend to think the worst of people and situations
	Projecting	I attribute my negative thoughts and emotions to others and take no responsibility for them
7	**Erratic**	I am unpredictable in my responses and reactions in any given moment
	Self-defeating	I act in a way that thwarts my own progress and interests
	Panicked	I am terrified of risks and too paralysed to act

Figure 18: Type 6 continuum – considered to self-defeating

Type 7: Visionary to scattered

Sevens bring joy, enthusiasm and optimism to life. They are engaged, versatile and adept, getting involved in and committing to making things better and bringing about positive outcomes. They are able to do a variety of things with equal ease and competence and can distil their broad experience of life into an effective path forward for others. They have a talent at rapidly seeing what's possible and, as those visions come easily to them, they can move towards those possibilities quickly.

> *Gift*: The gift of this type is the ability to envisage what is possible and inspire others through this.

> *Basic fear*: Being deprived and trapped in emotional pain.

> *Coping strategy*: Noticing options and opportunities and planning for the next pleasurable experience.

Sevens avoid looking at the negative side of life. They bring a deep and heartfelt happiness to everything and everyone around them and are able to savour deeply and feel great gratitude for what is here with them. Theirs is an optimism that believes there are no problems that can't be solved or situations that can't be fixed. They like to spend time remembering the good things in their lives and want others to see them as positively as they see themselves.

Sevens love to get other people involved in their plans and activities. They inspire others to fully experience and engage with their own potential. They have a preference for team responsibility and group decision making. They are the kind of people others like to have around, because they bring a lightness of spirit and a sense of happiness wherever they go.

Their difficulty comes in putting their ideas into action and in particular following through on their plans – especially in their personal lives. Sevens have a tendency to feel incapable of handling life, so will often procrastinate and not bring stressful situations to closure. They have difficulty reading the motives of others and, as a result, tend to presume the best of everyone and can therefore be gullible. They hide their feelings of incapability with social charm and good cheer; they live with the illusion that all emotional pain and sorrow in life can be eliminated by thinking positively and doing only those things that make you feel good.

Sevens are motivated to keep all options open, believing that 'the grass is greener' elsewhere – that there are better opportunities and situations to be pursued. Rather than commit to any one thing, they continuously search for new experiences and keep up a strong and positive excitement about things. The Seven's mind races at a hundred miles an hour with ideas and plans to make life easier and better. They develop highly analytical minds and are drawn to people and situations that stimulate them intellectually.

Sevens take great pleasure in pleasing others and making them happy. Their deep love for family and friends is evidenced in their lifelong loyalty. They constantly try to show others how much they care by doing small kind and thoughtful things, in part because they have difficulty expressing emotion directly. This is part of the secret serious side of Sevens that many people either miss altogether or take for granted.

The Seven's tendency towards light-hearted relationships diverts attention from their depth of character. As a consequence they may appear shallow. However, they would rather that you and they focus together on experiencing the positive side of life. This attitude is well summed up as: 'There is nothing you cannot enjoy, if you just put your mind to it'.

Type 7 and its emotional health continuum

Sevens with a higher level of emotional health are focused, disciplined, generative and productive. They are masterful and versatile, doing many things with great capability due to the variety of experiences they have had in their lives. They move into their visionary capacities, able to see possibilities and take action quickly for the sake of the community and others. They are grateful and appreciative of what they have.

At lower emotional health levels, Sevens become more frenetically busy, without the ability to slow down. They get scattered, pulled in many different directions and are unable to focus their attention on any one thing or person. They can become overindulgent without experiencing any satisfaction and they can be caught cutting corners, doing things quickly and expediently just to get them done. They can have a lack of concern about integrity, standards or doing things the right way. They can also display a strong unwillingness to deal with anything unpleasant or difficult, and a strong reframing reflex so that everything is seen in a positive light – even if it is not a positive situation. This can create a denial about what is really going on.

Figure 19 illustrates the continuum of type 7 personalities across the range of emotional health levels.

2	Joyful	I bring a deep and heartfelt happiness to everything around me
	Enthusiastic	I am joyous in creating wonderful possibilities with and for others
	Uplifting	I bring a positive spirit to those around me through my generosity and ease
3	Accomplished	I have a capacity for high quality work and exemplary delivery of multiple tasks and projects
	Versatile	I am able to do a variety of things with equal ease and competence
	Synthesizing	I bring together different strands of thinking and generate new and wonderful ideas and things
4	Seeking variety	I look for and engage in a range of options and new or different experiences
	Keeping options open	I continue to look for other possibilities and opportunities rather than commit
	Reframing	I ensure that whatever I say is always framed in a positive light
5	Rebellious	I am flippant and dismissive of rules and boundaries as I don't like to be limited
	Irreverent	I take nothing seriously and turn everything into a joke as a way of dealing with my anxieties and problems
	Hyperactive	I am constantly active and always looking for something new to amuse me so I won't get bored
6	Scattered	I am pulled in many different directions and cannot focus my attention
	Manic	I am frantically busy and cannot slow down
	Hedonistic	I overindulge in material pleasures, yet am unsatisfied by it all
7	Sensation seeking	I seek extreme excitement to avoid pain and commitment
	Escaping	I make sure that I never experience unpleasant situations
	Debauched	I live a life of excess in vices, pushing things to the limit

Figure 19: Type 7 continuum – visionary to scattered

Additional perspectives on Enneagram types

Given the complexity of the human personality, it is not surprising that there are numerous other perspectives we can draw on to understand the Enneagram types. In the following sections we look at a number of these and their relationships to emotional health. Other points of view provide additional information that can help us identify our dominant Enneagram type. Beyond that, these perspectives provide a stronger basis for identifying a development path towards increased emotional health.

The Hornevian groups (social styles): pursuing primary needs

One such approach is through the lens of how people of each type try to get their primary needs met.

Recall that those who tend to lean towards the body centre (Enneagram types 8, 9 and 1) have a primary need for autonomy; those who lean towards the heart centre (types 2, 3 and 4) have a primary need for attention; and those who lean towards the head centre (types 5, 6 and 7) have a primary need for security.

We know from our exploration of the individual Enneagram types that the three types within each centre display quite different personality traits in many areas. One of those differences is in what we call their 'social style'. There are three social styles, which are also called the Hornevian groups after psychoanalyst Karen Horney, whose work in the mid-twentieth century inspired this thinking. Those groups are 'assertive', 'withdrawn' and 'earning' (referred to as

HORNEVIANS	ATTENTION	SECURITY	AUTONOMY
ASSERTS	TYPE 3	TYPE 7	TYPE 8
WITHDRAWS	TYPE 4	TYPE 5	TYPE 9
EARNS	TYPE 2	TYPE 6	TYPE 1

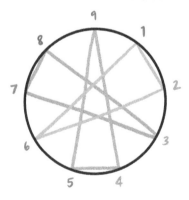

Figure 20: Table of Hornevian groups and the links between their Enneagram types

'dutiful' by some authors), and one Enneagram type from each centre is associated with each of these. This gives us three new triads, as illustrated in Figure 20.

This table should make it clearer how people from the same centre, with the same primary need, can pursue that need in quite different ways.

The assertive styles are very much focused on getting what they desire (whether that be attention, security or autonomy) and will step forward to achieve this. They see what they want and act on it. Threes are forthright in seeking the attention they desire. Sevens achieve security by being proactive. Eights don't hold back in 'doing it for themselves'.

The withdrawn types withdraw or move away from engagement with people to get what they want or need. In Fours, this often paradoxically means seeking attention in creative pursuits while maintaining mental solitude – imagine the actor who is exuberant on stage but highly introverted off it. For Fives, security comes from being on their own with their own thoughts. Nines can do the same, though their withdrawal can be mental rather than physical.

The earning types earn or do what is expected and/or required of them to get what they want or need. They are tuned into what they feel the world around them – whether that be their community, their workplace or society more broadly – needs them to do. Twos seek attention for themselves by providing attention to others. Sixes look for security through order and loyalty, through compliance with the 'way we do things around here'. Ones find autonomy by taking the lead in the pursuit of their causes.

So how is all this affected by emotional health?

At the higher emotional health levels (level 3 and higher) we are better able to use each of these social styles, or a mixture of them, in the same way that we have balanced access to all three centres. The mixture of social styles we use is based on conscious choices made in the context of the particular environment and circumstances we find ourselves in. Someone observing a person of high emotional health is unlikely to see one dominant social style in action.

At level 4, our awareness is such that we are conscious of the social style we prefer to use but can sometimes also make choices about using another style where appropriate. A keen observer will generally be able to identify a preference for two of the social styles over the third.

At level 5 we will predominantly use our preferred social style (that associated with our Enneagram type). We may be aware of the other two styles, while being less likely to use them under normal circumstances.

As we move down to level 6 we start to exaggerate the use of our preferred social style (again based on our Enneagram type) in order to have our primary need fulfilled. As an example, the assertive types (3, 7 and 8) can demand that they get what they want, potentially being (or at least appearing to be) aggressive in doing this. Those who are observing someone at this level will be able to identify the preferred social style in action without much difficulty. The further we go down the emotional health levels the stronger or more exaggerated our preferred social style becomes.

Recognising which social styles we use and when we use them, our attachment to one style over the others, and learning how we can start to access our less-preferred styles are all part of the development path towards increasing our emotional health level.

The Harmonic groups: when our primary needs are not met

The Harmonic groups offer another perspective on the Enneagram types. They complement the Hornevian groups in that while the Hornevians indicate how we get our primary needs met, the Harmonics indicate how we respond when we are not able to get those needs met. The Harmonics reveal the fundamental way that our personality defends against loss and disappointment.

The Harmonic groups are 'positive outlook', 'competent' and 'reactive', sometimes now referred to as 'emotionally real' (see Figure 21). As with the Hornevians, we find that each of these is associated with one Enneagram in each centre; however, the Harmonic groups are different from the Hornevian groups, creating an entirely different set of triads.

HARMONICS	ATTENTION	SECURITY	AUTONOMY
POSITIVE OUTLOOK	TYPE 2	TYPE 7	TYPE 9
COMPETENT	TYPE 3	TYPE 5	TYPE 1
EMOTIONALLY REAL/REACTIVE	TYPE 4	TYPE 6	TYPE 8

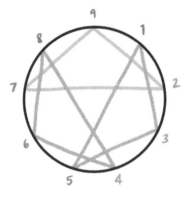

Figure 21: Table of Harmonic groups and the links between their Enneagram types

This time we can see how people from the same centre, with the same primary need, can respond differently to not having their need met.

The positive outlook group respond to conflict and difficulty by avoiding the situation, minimising it and reframing it in some positive way. These strategies allow them to maintain a positive outlook (while potentially failing to address the problem). Twos do this by maintaining their focus on others, perhaps giving them the illusion of receiving attention. For Sevens it's about trying to maintain outward enthusiasm. Nines epitomise the 'keep calm and carry on' mantra.

The competent group have learned to deal with difficulty by putting aside their personal feelings and emotions and striving to be effective, objective and competent in overcoming the challenge. For Threes this means minimising any effect on their reputation. Fives look to taking a wider view and accumulating more information and knowledge, while Ones tend to fall back on their fundamental beliefs in what's 'right' and 'just'.

The reactive (emotionally real) group react emotionally to conflicts and problems. They have a hard time containing their feelings, and this emotional intensity allows them to feel the 'realness' of the problem or issue. They want to know where others stand. Fours might express their emotions through their creativity – through art for instance – while Sixes can be acutely aware of others' reactions to their showing of emotion. Eights are less likely to hold back, their displays of emotion giving them the energy to confront the situation. We prefer to use the term 'emotionally real/reactive' for this group as it makes more sense in the context of emotional health. When someone in this Harmonic group acts below the line, they will be 'emotionally reactive'; when they act above the line, they will be more inclined to be 'emotionally real'. The term 'emotionally real/reactive' encompasses both states. When those in this group operate above the line, they are conscious of the passion they are bringing and look for this from others as well.

In terms of emotional health, in general when we are at a higher emotional health level (level 3 and higher) we tend to be able to access all of these responses, based on the environment and circumstances that surround us. Our access to all three centres means our responses become conscious choices, with no one Harmonic dominating.

At level 4 our awareness is such that we are conscious of the way we react to our primary need not being met but we can also make choices about reacting differently in particular circumstances. As with the Hornevian groups, an observer may be able to identify two of the styles that we tend to use more frequently.

At level 5 we predominantly use one of the Harmonic responses – the one associated with our dominant Enneagram type – when we are triggered. We tend not to use the others much at all. It's at this point that those in the 'emotionally real/reactive' Harmonic group will be more 'reactive' than 'real' as they display their emotions.

As we move down to level 6, we start to exaggerate the use of our preferred Harmonic response to defend against our loss and disappointment. The further we go down the emotional health levels the stronger or more exaggerated this response will be as part of our defence mechanism.

As with the Hornevians, recognising our attachment to a preferred Harmonic, knowing which we use and when and learning how we can start to access the others can be an important part of our development of our emotional health.

Shifting types: the stress and secure points

We're now in a position to explore the meaning of the arrows in the Enneagram diagram. They represent the internal dynamics of the Enneagram and can help us understand the ways in which our behaviour shifts when we are feeling particularly secure or, conversely, when we are feeling stressed.

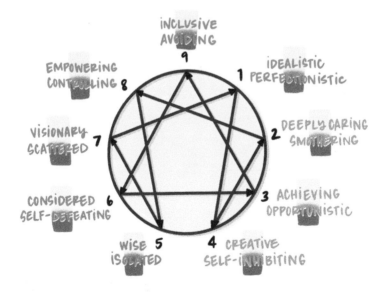

Figure 22: Enneagram showing emotional health continuum extremes

Figure 22 shows the Enneagram again, this time with the addition of the continuum extremes for each of the Enneagram types.

The 'stress point'

The direction of the arrow from your primary (or dominant) type indicates what we call the 'stress point' for that type. By 'stress' we are referring to how a person acts when they perceive their basic fear may be realised.

Let's take a person of type 5 as an example (Figure 23). Recall that a Five's basic fear is 'being incompetent, useless and incapable'. When a Five fears that they are failing in something they are doing, their behaviours will tend to move towards those more typical of a Seven. If our Five has an average to lower level of emotional health,

Figure 23: The 'stress point' for type 5 is type 7

they will likely display the sorts of behaviour associated at the lower end of the Seven's emotional health continuum, that is, towards the 'scattered' end. They will become hyperactive and distracted, just as a Seven tends to do if they act below the line. If our Five has a higher level of emotional health, fear of failure will cause them to become more visionary – to relax their high standards of evidence and look for alternative ways that might work.

It's worth noting that the pressure we feel at a time of stress can cause us to drop a level below our 'normal' level of emotional health before we move to our stress point.

Similarly, when a One is acting under stress, they will tend towards behaviours more characteristic of a Four in order to overcome their basic fear of being 'bad, defective or wrong'. An emotionally healthy One will become more creative than their type normally allows them to be, whereas a One of average to low emotional health will become uncharacteristically inhibited.

It should be noted that choosing to use the gift of our stress point will help us resolve the issue that sent us there in the first place.

The 'secure point'

At the tail end of the arrow pointing towards your dominant type (that is, 'against' the arrowhead) lies your 'secure point'. Secure refers to how we act when we perceive our basic fear may never be realised.

If we consider our type 5 person again (Figure 24), they will feel secure when they are feeling competent, useful and capable. When this is the case, their behaviours will tend to move towards those more typical of an Eight, that is, on the 'empowering' to 'controlling' continuum. Once again the specific behaviours our Five will display will depend on their emotional health level. A secure Five of average to low emotional health can become autocratic and demanding; a secure Five of high emotional health can become uncharacteristically self-confident, empowering and protective.

Figure 24: The 'secure point' for type 5 is type 8

The secure point for our One is type 7, the 'visionary' to 'scattered' that, interestingly, is also the stress point for our Five. When our One perceives that their basic fear of being 'bad, defective or wrong' won't be realised, their behaviours start to reflect those more typical of a Seven, that is, more visionary for those with a higher level of emotional health to more scattered and impulsive (that is, letting go of some of their perfectionist tendencies) for those with lower emotional health.

Stress points and understanding your type

Knowing more about the dynamics of the stress point can also assist you in coming closer to identifying your primary Enneagram type.

For example, if your original assessment of your own Enneagram type(s) using the process described on page 57 indicates that you have two strong Enneagram types, following the direction of the arrows away from those two types and exploring the corresponding stress points (and thinking about the way you behave under stress) might help you see a clearer preference for one of these types over the other.

For instance, let's say you are strong in both type 7 and type 3.

We can see that the stress point for a Seven is type 1. Type 1 behaviours are where a Seven will typically move when they perceive their basic fear – of being trapped in emotional pain – is about to be realised. With this in mind, look at the type 1 emotional health continuum (idealistic to perfectionist) illustrated on page 73 and identify those behaviours that are most like you under stress. If type 1 is in fact your stress point, you are likely to be able to identify a number of your own behaviours on this continuum, and they will generally be those in the range of emotional health levels 4 to 6. If on further reflection you find that you definitely relate to these behaviours in stressful situations then it may be that type 1 is your stress point, which would reinforce type 7 as your primary type.

By contrast, the stress point for a Three is type 9. When a Three perceives their basic fear – of being worthless and of having no value apart from one's achievements – is about to be realised they will move towards type 9. With this in mind, you can repeat the process outlined in the previous paragraph, only this time for the type 9 emotional health continuum (inclusive to avoiding) on page 69. Once again, identify any behaviours on this list that are most like you when you are under stress. If you have selected a number of these behaviours (again that are likely to be those the range of emotional health levels from 4 to 6) – and in particular more than you did for type 1 – and if on further reflection you definitely relate to these behaviours in stressful situations, this would indicate that type 9 is more of your stress point than type 1. This would reinforce type 3 as a primary type for you over type 7.

Of course, you can apply this same comparison to any other types that you feel are candidates to be your primary type.

Please note that while this process can provide another step in getting closer to identifying your primary Enneagram type, it will not be effective for everyone. We find that some people who lead quite safe lives rarely if ever move to their stress point simply because they avoid becoming stressed. The same applies to those with a high emotional health level. Because they have an increased range of behavioural freedom and broader possible responses to situations they find themselves in, they tend to move to their stress point less often than others. On the other hand, there are some people who can't recognise when they are at their stress point as their level of self-awareness is not sufficient for them to understand that their behaviours change under stress. This is particularly common in those with a low level of emotional health.

In addition, this stress-and-secure-point methodology will only work in helping to identify your primary type. When exploring your other types you are unlikely to see their associated stress- and security-point behaviours or characteristics in yourself.

The instinctual variants

The instinctual variants (sometimes referred to as instinctual drives) are primal to us as human beings. They reside in our body centre and are very much part of our physical makeup. There are three instinctual variants and each of us possesses all of them. In those with average emotional health, one of the three dominates, one is secondary and the third is under-utilised. This relative dominance has a strong influence on our behaviours while at the same time remaining independent of our Enneagram type.

The three instinctual variants are:
- self-preservation
- social
- sexual.

Those with a dominant self-preservation instinct are preoccupied with getting and maintaining physical safety and comfort. On entering a room these people notice the temperature of the room, where the heater is, where the food and refreshments are, where is a good place to sit, etc. They are quick to comment if any of the environmental elements are not meeting their needs. As individuals they generally don't display a lot of radiant energy; in fact, some seem to absorb the energy of others in the room.

Those with a dominant social instinct are preoccupied with being liked, approved of and feeling safe with others. On entering a room these people notice who is talking with the host, who has power or prestige, or who might be able to help them. They generally display a diffused radiant energy in many directions at once, for instance to a group of people as opposed to an individual.

Those with a dominant sexual instinct are preoccupied with connecting with others for intense contact and experiences. On entering a room these people notice where the most attractive and interesting people are. They are very focused on one-to-one relationships. They generally display an intense and focused radiant energy directed at one or two individuals.

The instinctual variants are different to the so-called 'subtypes'. Because there are three instinctual variants and nine Enneagram types, some authors describe the product of the two in terms of twenty-seven separate subtypes (e.g. the 'self-preservation type 4', the 'social type 4' and the 'sexual type 4', and so on for each

Enneagram type). A large part of the influence that the instinctual variants have on Enneagram type comes from the energy each of the instinctual variants brings, along with the way in which each type responds to that energy. The energy relating to each instinctual variant can work with or against the energy levels of a specific Enneagram type. Other characteristics of the instinctual variants also affect each type differently.

It's beyond the scope of this book to go deeply into the detail of each instinctual variant/Enneagram subtype (let alone the variations of each with different emotional health levels). Other authors have already contributed significantly to this discussion and in some depth. Instead we will focus on basic descriptions of the three variants at a conceptual level, their effect on those with an average emotional health level and their link to emotional health levels and emotional health development.

The instinctual variants and emotional health

Similar to the centres of intelligence, when we have a higher level of emotional health we tend to have a greater balance and integration of the three instinctual variants, with no one instinct dominating. This integration enables us to maintain our 'being' at the higher levels.

At emotional health level 4, we have access to all three instinctual variants; however, we generally find one is more dominant and one of the other two is given preference over the third. We are able to start accessing the gifts and strategies of those that are not our preference as our circumstances require. We have sufficient self-awareness to make these choices.

When we are at level 5, we use and identify with our dominant instinct in most of what we do. We tend to only use the other instincts to fulfil certain needs that we see as important to us at the time.

When we are at level 6, we start to overuse our dominant instinctual variant. We may access components of the other instinctual variants when we feel doing so is necessary to fulfil our primary needs, but we likely won't be aware that this is happening: it isn't something we are choosing to do.

The instinctual variants and their influence are important to understand if we want to develop and move up the emotional health levels. We need to understand which one we are attached to and which we are not using and why. Overcoming these patterns and blocks is essential to achieving the balance and integration of the instincts that characterise higher levels of emotional health. Balance in the three instinctual variants enables us to fully access the three centres and also let go of our patterns of behaviours.

While we have a preference for developing our understanding of the core elements of each instinctual variant and then applying and exploring this within ourselves (bringing greater self-awareness), we acknowledge that sometimes it is easier to read detailed descriptions of the impact of each of the instinctual variants on each Enneagram type individually to help identify what we are most like. Our caution here is to avoid becoming too attached to a specific description of 'who you are' and instead use this knowledge to assist you in overcoming your current biases and attachments. Of course, as you develop a greater degree of behavioural freedom and with it a more balanced use of all three instinctual variants and the nine Enneagram types (that is, as you improve your emotional health level), the specific descriptions of each variant/Enneagram subtype will become less relevant in any case.

Responses to change

Just as the Hornevian and Harmonic groups, stress and secure points, and the instinctual variants can affect us differently depending on our dominant Enneagram type, preferred centre of intelligence and emotional health level, so too can change. As a general rule, humans like stability. The widespread aversion to change is on show in offices, homes and wider society every day, every time something changes, from the design of our bank notes to the traffic-light sequence at a busy intersection. The advent of social media makes this aversion starker, as even the smallest change can cause a flurry of negative posts.

As we have previously discussed, each of us has a basic fear which (at average emotional health levels) drives a coping strategy that 'jumps into action' whenever we perceive this fear is about to be realised. Change immediately puts us on high alert as we try to assess the extent to which it might realise our basic fear. We often find ourselves holding a 'silent question' in the back of our minds – a subconscious test of our readiness to cope with the change. The way we perceive the answer to that question will determine our response to the change. Again, at average emotional health levels, this all takes place automatically. Sometimes – but not necessarily – it may also involve moving to our stress point.

Our silent question and our coping strategies are long held, emerging as they do from the primary Enneagram type we were probably born with. They affect our thoughts, feelings and actions about change – unless we consciously bring them into our awareness.

At higher emotional health levels, with a more active inner observer, we are able to recognise the silent question we are holding in the face of change. When we are conscious of the silent question, notice it and acknowledge it as a component of our coping strategy, we can shift our perception and understanding of what is happening and create an alternative response. In the moment of awareness, we have choice: we can choose a state we desire.

The following are brief summaries of each Enneagram type's response to change, including the silent question they hold and the way they respond.

Type 8

At average emotional health levels, an Eight who is faced with change is likely to hold a silent question around, 'Who or what is trying to control me?' The question comes from a desire to check whether the chosen route is something they can control or that could otherwise make them vulnerable. They will withdraw and analyse what is happening before either fully committing themselves to the change or fighting against it. Once they decide their path, they will take things in hand energetically so as not to waste time; they will dismiss feelings and vulnerability in the process, as these are seen to get in the way.

At higher emotional health levels, Eights will seek to integrate multiple points of view, looking for paths forward that will enable and empower others as well as themselves to work with the change rather than against it. They will also acknowledge their own feelings and vulnerabilities around the change and share these with others.

Type 9

At average emotional health levels, a Nine faced with change is likely to be torn between the conflicting responses of others to the change, silently asking, 'Do I really want to be drawn into this?' They can see all the possible advantages and disadvantages involved and will attempt to alleviate tensions (both in themselves and others) by listening to everyone.

This Nine's doubts and worries often cause them to create worst-case scenarios and they look for guidance and support outside themselves as a result. With all of this information in hand, they might start to go down one path, only to find themselves under pressure from someone with another perspective and path. This will cause the Nine to remain stuck in their indecision.

At higher emotional health levels, Nines will add their own perspective to the advantages and disadvantages of the change and look to find a harmonious and inclusive way forward from all that they heard. They are able to mediate differences of opinion to find agreed solutions and pay attention to their own needs and feelings around the change as part of this.

Type 1

At average emotional health levels, a One's first reaction to a planned change will likely be to see all the faults in it and silently ask, 'How can I prove that I am right?' Ones come to believe that their opinion is generally closest to the 'right way' to move forward. They see themselves as having worked through the situation in a rational and logical way, so others should listen to their plan as a result.

They will be doubtful about anyone else's suggestions to overcome the faults they perceive, regarding those proposals as rushed and having not been thought through. They would like other people to take account of their (the One's) opinion; they want others to support their own concerns with evidence rather than simply 'complaining' about the change or offering suggestions that haven't been validated.

Ones with a higher level of emotional health will accept that no plan for change can be perfect and that leading others through the change, rather than expecting to control it or them, is what will more likely work. They are open to possibilities and look at what can be achieved in the change rather than what is wrong with it.

Type 2

At average emotional health levels, Twos are likely to feel the impact that a change will have on others. They immediately hold the silent question, 'How can I help and offer my availability to others?', regardless of how the change may affect them.

In putting others' needs ahead of their own, these Twos neglect to check in with their own feelings and emotions around the change. They believe that if they are looking out for others, they will ultimately be looked after themselves. Unfortunately, this is often not the outcome they experience and they are left feeling excluded and 'worn out' as a result.

At higher emotional health levels, Twos will bring a more balanced approach to change, focusing on themselves as well as on the needs of others. They explore the desired outcomes of the change and what it will look like for themselves and others, then build strategies to strengthen interdependence rather than dependence.

Type 3

At average emotional health levels, a Three is likely to immediately seize opportunities associated with a change as they respond to their silent question, 'How do I get you to notice me and what I am doing?' They turn these opportunities into actions long before others have even come to terms with what is changing.

Wanting to appear successful regardless of what is happening, these Threes disengage from feelings and reality and move into 'performing'. As a result, they dismiss their own and others' concerns about and reactions to the change. This can result in burnout and neglect.

At higher emotional health levels, Threes will direct their attention to the health and wellbeing of both themselves and others in dealing with the change, as well as looking for efficient and effective ways of working with and through it. Realistic deadlines, consultation around the 'what and how' of change and appreciation of effort and achievement are all present.

Type 4

At average emotional health levels, a Four is likely to approach a change with a silent question, 'Why does no one appreciate the feelings and emotions inherent in the situation?' They point to the history of the affected organisation or community in order to demonstrate that 'people' – by which they mean themselves – are poorly understood with regard to their aspirations. They will argue that it is time to devise more creative solutions to the problems posed.

The expression of these thoughts will tend to be dramatic and emotionally exaggerated, which can be confusing to others, as the Four will provide little information about what their solutions look like or what their proposed next steps are. The Four's response is more about how no one understands them and what they could bring to the change if given the opportunity.

At higher emotional health levels, Fours experience and express their emotions in a clear and centred way that encourages others to feel more open and comfortable about sharing what they are experiencing as well. They apply their creative approaches to change in order to expand the thinking of others around what is possible and how they can all work together for personal and organisational or community success.

Type 5

At average emotional health levels a Five is likely to withdraw from conversations around a change with a silent question around 'What more do I need to know?' They will reflect (alone) on the issues and consequences of what is happening. The Five's desire to remain competent and capable, regardless of the change, creates a need to distance themselves from feelings and vulnerability – both personally and in others.

Because of this, the Five can come across to others as cold, disinterested and dismissive of their needs or feelings around the change. The Five's need to be seen to be competent by bringing knowledge and expertise to the change only adds to this perspective.

At higher emotional health levels, Fives will share their time, knowledge, space and stories around a change in order to fully engage with others. People will know and understand what they appreciate and find difficult about the change as well. The knowledge and expertise the Five brings is shared with others in order to find solutions and opportunities.

Type 6

At average emotional health levels, Sixes confronted with change will tend to wonder about the true intentions of those who have made decisions about the change. They will hold a silent question, 'Am I going to be okay here?' They will work to verify this by cross-checking the information they have been given previously.

Their constant questioning and their defending and justifying of current processes and practices can cause others to avoid involving them in planning for the change. This in turn causes the Six to increase their vigilance around the change, developing numerous scenarios related to it so as not to be caught off guard. They become mistrusting, confused and stuck in their own thinking, the change becoming more overwhelming and overpowering as a result.

At higher emotional health levels, the Six has the capability to meet life's challenges as they can see both the consequences of and solutions in most change. They proactively troubleshoot with the change makers, bringing different scenarios and perspectives into the mix that enable the effective implementation of the change.

Type 7

At average emotional health levels, a Seven confronted with change holds the silent question, 'How do I move on?' They are likely to already be getting bored with existing routines, so can quickly see the interesting and exciting possibilities that a change might bring.

Not wanting to get trapped into precise roles, or have to deal with uncomfortable experiences too quickly, this Seven makes sure they add their own expansive thinking to the way the change could be achieved. At the same time they avoid committing to taking action or developing a plan themselves. This can leave others to see them as scattered, uncommitted and lacking responsibility, which can lead to them losing opportunities to lead and engage others with their inspiring pictures of the future.

At higher emotional health levels, the Seven is able to bring the generative and visionary thinking required in any change and make it both exciting and feasible. They integrate the more uncomfortable facets of change by sustaining a focus on its implementation and inspiring and engaging others to do the same.

Part 3:
Development paths to building emotional health

AT THE BEGINNING of this book we described the Enneagram as a powerful tool to support you in your journey of self-discovery and vertical development, providing you with insights into your own personality, behaviour and emotional health and into the way you interact with others. We trust that we've also left you with a sense of what you can aspire to in terms of creating an emotionally healthy balance in all nine types which, as we mentioned in an earlier section, is our ultimate emotional health development goal.

It's important to understand that moving up the emotional health levels and remaining 'above the line' at all times, or even most of the time, cannot be achieved by simply 'thinking' about doing so. Central to increasing your emotional health are:

- developing your inner observer to become increasingly aware of your automated responses and their impact on others

- understanding what drives and motivates your behaviour and why this is the case, including in different circumstances such as being stressed or feeling secure, or not having your basic needs met, and

- consciously choosing, and taking, development paths that move you towards lower self-centredness, a higher degree of behavioural freedom and, in turn, whole body thinking and 'presence'.

There are fundamentally two pathways of development: the psychological and the somatic. Both of these will be covered in this section, along with the 'imbalance of the centres' which provides a connection between these two pathways.

The first chapter below addresses psychological development. By that we are referring to understanding our own psychology, and in particular the patterns we get caught up in as a result of our personality.

To achieve any substantial vertical development we must, as we said earlier in this book, 'let go of limits on our thinking and perceptions'. In other words, we need to recognise the patterns we get caught up in and find ways to escape or change those patterns. This starts with understanding the components of our personality we have described in the first two parts of this book.

We initially offer development pathways for each Enneagram type as a starting point to help you create a development journey that is right for you. The next step is to apply a broader level of understanding of our own unique combination of those things that drive and motivate us, expressed through what we think, feel and do.

For this reason it's important to find a combination of strategies that is relevant to your own personal development path. This will include bringing into the mix an understanding of the effects on your personality of the additional perspectives on the Enneagram types, including the Hornevian and Harmonic groups, the impact of stress and security, the instinctual variants and the responses to change. These different perspectives will probably make the 'standard' development path for your Enneagram type a bit fuzzier as they identify more pathways. On the other hand, mixing and matching some of the techniques for each of the nine types – especially those associated with your type by one of the various lines we've shown on the Enneagram diagram – will help bring the picture of your development pathway into clearer focus. Ultimately, we encourage you to try any of the strategies below that feels right for you, rather than just focusing on the ideas that are provided for your stronger types.

In the next chapter, entitled 'The imbalance of the centres', we dive more deeply into the relationships between the centres of intelligence and each of the Enneagram types, how these change with emotional health level and, in turn, how you can use this knowledge to further refine your development path.

Psychological development
Breaking out of the patterns you get caught in

Bringing our thoughts, feelings and senses into our 'conscious now' is one of the greatest challenges we face. Being aware of why we do what we do gives us the power to make changes to how we think, feel and do (behave). We need to have a conscious focus on the impact we are having on those around us, and this only comes through self-awareness and effective use of our inner observer.

As you start on this journey for yourself – as you start to build an understanding of why you do what you do – you will find that the depth of your self-awareness starts to increase. That is, as you start to be critically more self-reflective, you will notice more and more patterns you would like to change.

Imagine walking into a large room with a number of closed doors. As you open each of these you find another behaviour or pattern that you would like to change in yourself. This all seems quite manageable until you open the last door, only to find that you've entered another room, much larger than the last one, and with many, many more doors.

The realisation that the scope you have for improving yourself is never-ending can feel overwhelming, but you need to understand that you are only seeing these new doors because a new and higher level of self-awareness has brought us to this point. This awareness is allowing you to see many more opportunities for growth that you did not – in fact could not – recognise before.

To support you on this path, we encourage you to find someone you can talk to about it and who can help in your exploration. Ideally it will be someone who is also on the journey or who has been through it. (Feel free to contact us and we can put you in touch with such a person.) Continue to work through these new doors, even as more appear. Rest assured that the effort will be worth it.

Type 8 psychological development guide

'I step in and take charge.'

8

If we summarise what we know so far about type 8 it looks like this:

Gift	The gift of Eights is the ability to bring genuine human strength and courage when facing whatever needs to be confronted. People with this gift are resourceful, decisive and self-reliant, dealing with difficult situations cleverly and effectively, without giving up or backing down.
Basic fear	Being harmed or controlled by others and thus becoming vulnerable.
Coping strategy	Exerting their will in order to remain strong and in charge of their life and those of others.
Centre of intelligence	Body
Primary need	Autonomy
Hornevian group*	Assert
Harmonic group†	Emotionally real/reactive
Stress point	Type 5 (wise to isolated)
Secure point	Type 2 (deeply caring to smothering)
Silent question	'Who or what is trying to control me?'

* how they try to get their primary need met
† response to not having primary need met

8

As with all the other types, the Eight's personality is further affected by their instinctual variant – self-preservation, social or sexual – which is independent of their type or the other factors listed above.

And of course the Eight's behaviours and their responses to situations in which they find themselves will depend on their level of emotional health.

Improving emotional health for the Eight

Let's now look at what this means in terms of the Eight who wants to increase their level of emotional health.

We know that Eights with an average level of emotional health are prone to be dominant. 'I am stronger than others and take control of situations and people around me.' They can also be blunt and controlling, some might say 'bossy'.

You can see in behaviours such as these, elements of the assertive in trying to get their primary need for autonomy met by being in control (Hornevian), elements of emotionally real/reactive when they perceive they are being controlled by others (Harmonic) and even as they isolate themselves to work out what they need to do to stay in control (stress point). Their response to change translates their need for autonomy into taking control of the situation so that nothing can control them.

In contrast we know that Eights who have a high level of emotional health are able to surrender their need for control. They retain their ability to make things happen, but now they are able to do so while also empowering others and acknowledging their own feelings and limitations. 'Stepping back so others can step forward.' Eights with a high emotional health level are very good at 'making it all happen' while bringing others with them in the process and building shared confidence along the way.

8

To start to move up the emotional health levels as an Eight, you must learn to reclaim your tender side and put this into practice. This is essential for your long-term wellbeing. You need to share your vulnerabilities and trust that others are able to take control of situations. You must also learn to be more receptive and responsive to input from others rather than moving to immediate, unilateral action.

Some of the actions you can take include:

- Practise pausing before reacting or taking action.

- Practise real listening and negotiation and improve your ability to do both.

- Choose your battles by looking at the possible consequences or fallout and letting the small stuff go.

- Practise asking permission and avoid bulldozing your way through with your own determination.

- Channel your passion and energy and direct it carefully.

- Get comfortable showing your vulnerable side; compassion and empathy are sources of strength.

8

Strengthening your connection to type 8, as a non-Eight

To strengthen this area if you don't have a strong connection to it, you need to build the capability to 'step in' to situations and work through what is needed without hesitating or continually relying on others to provide you with feedback. Go first, step forward instead of waiting, notice what it feels like when you get things done quickly.

You can start by ensuring that you have the 'bigger picture' in mind; that is, identify what is expected to be achieved, what the desired outcomes are and the likely impact on the organisation. Then tap into the talent around you to make it all happen.

Type 9 psychological development guide

'I blend in and stay calm.'

9

If we summarise what we know so far about type 9 it looks like this:

Gift	The gift of Nines is the ability to bring a sense of peace and harmony to all situations. They are patient and diplomatic, able to find common ground and solutions, see multiple perspectives and engage others in dialogue around these.
Basic fear	Being lost or 'separated from oneself'.
Coping strategy	Forgetting themselves and seeking belonging.
Centre of intelligence	Body
Primary need	Autonomy
Hornevian group*	Withdraw
Harmonic group†	Positive outlook
Stress point	Type 6 (considered to be self-defeating)
Secure point	Type 3 (achieving to opportunistic)
Silent question	'Do I really want to be drawn into this?'

* how they try to get their primary need met
† response to not having primary need met

9

Again, as with the other types, the Nine's personality is further affected by their instinctual variant – self-preservation, social or sexual – which is independent of their type or the other factors listed above.

And of course the Nine's behaviours and their responses to situations in which they find themselves will depend on their level of emotional health.

Improving emotional health for the Nine

Let's now look at what this means in terms of the Nine who wants to increase their level of emotional health.

Nines with an average level of emotional health tend to be easygoing, neutral and accommodating, preferring to avoid confrontation where they can. 'I oblige and give in to others even if it's not what I really want.' They don't invest in any particular outcome and they can also have a habit of procrastinating or being indecisive.

You can see in behaviours such as these, elements of the withdrawn in trying to get their primary need for autonomy met (Hornevian), moving to a positive outlook when that isn't happening (Harmonic) and as they become self-defeating and simply unable to progress (stress point). Their response to change translates their need for autonomy into not getting involved or engaged in the change at all.

9

In contrast, Nines with a high level of emotional health are more at ease with claiming their place and showing their 'quiet' strength. They bring a strong sense of peace and harmony to any situation but, rather than withdrawing into themselves, they work with and engage others in making them feel comfortable and at ease. They value others' contributions and are naturally inclusive, even drawn to mediation and finding consensus. They are resolute and have an inner determination that allows them to constructively overcome challenges that would commonly be avoided by the Nine with lower emotional health.

To move up the emotional health levels as a Nine, you must learn to express your thoughts, needs and preferences, even when these might oppose the wishes of others. You need to become active and assertive rather than acting in a passive way, learning to embrace conflict and deal with it directly, with the understanding that differences bring people together.

Some of the actions you can take include:

- Prioritise the things you need to do and then spend your time on your highest priorities.

- Tell others ... take a stand, give your opinion, make decisions, give clear guidance.

- Don't apologise or qualify your comments – be specific and direct.

WORKING WITH EMOTIONAL HEALTH AND THE ENNEAGRAM

9

- Don't work too hard to solve other people's problems.

- Narrow your focus – don't let your big-picture thinking lead to 'scope creep'.

- Take credit, authority and responsibility – don't give them away.

Strengthening your connection to type 9, as a non-Nine

To strengthen this area if you don't have a strong connection to it, you need to build the capability to feel grounded and connected to the world around you and those in it. Learn to listen to and appreciate the multiple perspectives that people can bring to a problem, topic or idea and find the connecting and binding threads that will bring people together to a common way forward.

You can start by beginning to listen without knowing, judging or interrupting – valuing the contribution each person is making – and sharing what you have heard and the impact it has on your thinking at that time.

Type 1 psychological development guide

'I judge and critique.'

If we summarise what we know so far about type 1 it looks like this:

Gift	The gift of Ones is the ability to see clearly what constitutes the good, the just, the right and the proper.
Basic fear	Being bad, defective or wrong.
Coping strategy	Seeing what is wrong and needing to correct it; perfectionism.
Centre of intelligence	Body
Primary need	Autonomy
Hornevian group*	Earn
Harmonic group†	Competent
Stress point	Type 4 (creative to self-inhibiting)
Secure point	Type 7 (visionary to scattered)
Silent question	'How can I prove that I'm right?'

* how they try to get their primary need met
† response to not having primary need met

1

As with the other types, the One's personality is further affected by their instinctual variant – self-preservation, social or sexual – which is independent of their type or the other factors listed above.

The One's level of emotional health will also affect their behaviours and their responses to situations in which they find themselves.

Improving emotional health for the One

Let's now look at what this means in terms of the One who wants to increase their level of emotional health.

We know that Ones of average emotional health tend to feel obligated: they notice their flaws and always feel they need to do more to improve themselves and they are always self-assessing their own actions to ensure they are 'acceptable'. 'I must strive higher and improve everything, including myself, others and the environment.'

You can see in behaviours such as these, elements of earning in trying to get their primary need for autonomy met (Hornevian), striving to what is right and is expected when that isn't happening (Harmonic) and brooding and becoming dramatic about not being good enough (stress point). Their response to change translates their need for autonomy into an expectation that others will accept their opinions.

At higher levels of emotional health, Ones know that there is more than one right way and that perfection is in the eyes of the

1

beholder. They are flexible, relaxed and non-judgemental, embracing opportunities to better understand others' perspectives. While the One's conscience and principles prevail, their desire to engage and involve others brings entirely new ways of creating an ideal way forward.

To move up the emotional health levels, the One must learn to become accepting rather than trying to make everything perfect. They need to learn to let go of being overly attentive to details and needing to have everything under control; they need to practise being more flexible and relaxed, less judgemental and reactive.

Some of the actions you can take include:

- Be a model rather than a critic.

- Practise checking the context of a situation before you offer ideas to improve it.

- Express yourself. Don't keep your feelings repressed.

- Appreciate the perfection of messes, mistakes and flaws – they are the birthplace of innovation and creativity.

- Practise asking whether it is more important to you to be right or to actually achieve the desired outcome?

- Learn to recognise the voice of your inner judge and to question its 'authority'.

- Turn your inner critic into an inner coach

1

Strengthening your connection to type 1, as a non-One

To strengthen this area if you don't have a strong connection to it, you need to reflect on what is important to you and what you will not compromise on in the way you live your life. As you explore these ideas, you will gain greater perspectives of your own principles and ways of engaging and better understand the impact these have on both you and others.

You can start by noticing what you are good at, what you bring and what you contribute rather than focusing on areas for improvement. Recognising the contributions you are already making will enable you to focus on what you are doing well, rather than what you need to do differently.

Type 2 psychological development guide

'I continually give to others.'

2

If we summarise what we know so far about type 2 it looks like this:

Gift	The gift of Twos is the ability to deeply empathise with others and be genuinely unselfish and compassionate in serving their needs.
Basic fear	Being unloved and unwanted.
Coping strategy	Focusing on others' needs, assuming they will get their own met through giving to and being wanted by others.
Centre of intelligence	Heart
Primary need	Attention
Hornevian group*	Earn
Harmonic group[†]	Positive outlook
Stress point	Type 8 (empowering to controlling)
Secure point	Type 4 (creative to self-inhibiting)
Silent question	'How can I help and be available to others?'

* how they try to get their primary need met
[†] response to not having primary need met

2

Again, the Two's instinctual variant – self-preservation, social or sexual (which is independent of their type or the other factors listed above) – further affects their personality.

The Two's level of emotional health will also affect their behaviours and their responses to situations in which they find themselves.

Improving emotional health for the Two

Let's now look at what this means in terms of the Two who wants to increase their level of emotional health.

At an average level of emotional health, the Two tends to be possessive in their 'need to be needed'. In their quest to be important to others they can become intrusive, while they can also be self-sacrificing. 'I overburden myself, helping too many people and feeling burdened as a result.'

You can see in behaviours such as these, elements of earning in trying to get their primary need for attention/validation met (Hornevian), maintaining a positive outlook when that isn't happening and continuing to pursue attention when others signal that they should perhaps step away (Harmonic) and in moving to 'controlling' in order to become more obvious (stress point). Their response to change translates their need for attention into putting their own feelings aside and automatically assuming that others need their care and attention more.

2

Twos at high emotional health levels recognise that while strong relationships are important, they also need to take care of themselves in the process. They understand that their self-worth is not solely attached to others loving or liking them. They still have a strong drive to nurture and care for others and will often seem to do so effortlessly, often recognised as natural coaches as a result. The difference at the higher level of emotional health is that they do this while genuinely engaging their interest in and concern for other people. They are no longer disguising their self-need under the cover of apparent concern for others.

To move up the emotional health levels as a Two, you must learn to stay connected to yourself. You need to learn to acknowledge that you have needs and desires and so focus more on taking care of yourself and less on catering to what you believe others need. You must learn to discern when your giving to others is appropriate and when it is not.

Some of the actions you can take include:

- If people aren't responding to your offers of help, step back and step away rather than doubling down in your efforts, in the belief that you will eventually be appreciated.

- Offer to help only when you really want to – stop keeping score.

- Ask for what you want – don't assume that others can read you as well as you can read them.

2

- Take time to reflect on your needs and what you need to do to take care of yourself.

- Learn to accept praise without discounting it.

- Recognise that not all problems are solved by focusing on relationships.

Strengthening your connection to type 2, as a non-Two

To strengthen this area if you don't have a strong connection to it you need to develop more connection to your heart. This means building stronger and closer relationships with more people. It is about developing a truly caring and compassionate connection with more than just those few people who are close to you. It is about expanding this connection to all with whom you come in contact.

You can start simply by showing an interest in what others are doing, thinking and feeling. Perhaps even developing a curiosity about others, their lives and all that this encompasses. Remember to also take care of yourself.

Type 3 psychological development guide

'I achieve impressive goals and tasks.'

If we summarise what we know so far about type 3 it looks like this:

Gift	The gift of Threes is the ability to bring energy, talent and organisation to make things happen and deliver results.
Basic fear	Being worthless and having no value apart from one's achievements.
Coping strategy	Accomplishing tasks and goals in the most efficient and expedient way to gain the attention of others.
Centre of intelligence	Heart
Primary need	Attention
Hornevian group*	Assert
Harmonic group†	Competent
Stress point	Type 9 (inclusive to avoiding)
Secure point	Type 6 (considered to self-defeating)
Silent question	'How do I get you to notice me and what I am doing?'

* how they try to get their primary need met
† response to not having primary need met

3

Again, the Three's instinctual variant – self-preservation, social or sexual (which is independent of their type or the other factors listed above) – further affects their personality.

The Three's level of emotional health will also affect their behaviours and their responses to situations in which they find themselves.

Improving emotional health for the Three

Let's now look at what this means in terms of the Three who wants to increase their level of emotional health.

Threes with an average level of emotional health are competitive and expedient. 'I want to be the winner, so I have to do better than others in all areas of my life.' They are also a chameleon, quick to change their colours to suit a situation in order to present themselves in the best light and be seen to be better than others.

You can see in behaviours such as these, elements of quickly asserting themselves in order to meet their primary need for attention (Hornevian), emphasising and even exaggerating their achievements and having competent responses to get the attention they need (Harmonic) and as they withdraw from the limelight when they see others as 'better' than them (stress point). Their response to change translates their need for attention into being dismissive of others' feelings and concerns in the face of change.

At high emotional health levels, Threes recognise that their

3

personal value is not wholly attached to the outcomes they achieve and that they are valued for who they are as a person as well as their successes. They engage others with ease and encouragement and are gracious in recognition, attributing success and outcomes to others as well as recognising the part they have played.

To move up the emotional health levels as a Three, you must learn to discover your true self and be willing to step past the image you hold of yourself. It is about recognising your capabilities and talents as they genuinely are and learning to explore your inner thoughts, feelings and experiences in order to become more authentic. You must learn to go with the flow of events and experiences and be less driven to make things happen all the time.

Some of the actions you can take include:

- Empower others to handle more than just the details.

- Expect people to voice objections and concerns – appreciate their need for stability and security. Not everyone is comfortable moving as quickly as you like to.

- Notice your tendency to close discussions too quickly. Do you really have enough information? Could you consider a few more variables? Ask 'What if ...?'

- Learn how to tell the difference between what you do and who you are.

3

- Make time for people – things get done by humans who need to connect with you.

- Practise authenticity. 'How are you?' is sometimes a genuine enquiry.

Strengthening your connection to type 3, as a non-Three

To strengthen this area if you don't have a strong connection to it, you need to focus on setting goals and achieving them, while at the same time engaging others and taking them on the journey. Understanding how you can use the talents and capabilities of others through networking and getting to know them can sometimes feel uncomfortable; however, this is a key step in building an achieving style. Accepting recognition for what you do and who you are is also an important growth area.

You can start by setting small, achievable goals and time frames and planning out the most effective and efficient way to attain them. Ask others for their ideas and guidance, which will build their interest and engagement. Increase the goals to larger and more complex tasks. Hold yourself accountable for achieving the results and time frames.

Type 4 psychological development guide

'I search for what is unique and special.'

If we summarise what we know so far about type 4 it looks like this:

Gift	The gift of Fours is the ability to appreciate the true beauty and uniqueness in people, things and the world around them.
Basic fear	Not having any identity or personal significance.
Coping strategy	Searching for the ideal – in love, in others and in the world around them.
Centre of intelligence	Heart
Primary need	Attention
Hornevian group*	Withdraw
Harmonic group†	Emotionally real/reactive
Stress point	Type 2 (deeply caring to smothering)
Secure point	Type 1 (idealistic to perfectionistic)
Silent question	'Why does no one appreciate the feelings and emotions in this situation?'

* how they try to get their primary need met
† response to not having primary need met

4

As with all types, the Four's instinctual variant – self-preservation, social or sexual (which is independent of their type or the other factors listed above) – further affects their personality.

The Four's level of emotional health will also affect their behaviours and their responses to situations in which they find themselves.

Improving emotional health for the Four

Let's now look at what this means in terms of the Four who wants to increase their level of emotional health.

At average emotional health levels, Fours have a tendency to be moody and brooding. 'I replay negative feelings from the past and return to them again and again.' They often feel inadequate and misunderstood, and they can be temperamental and sensitive – and expect that others will respect their sensitivity.

You can see in behaviours such as these, elements of withdrawing and becoming mysterious in order to meet their primary need for attention (Hornevian), becoming overly expressive and dramatic when that attention is not forthcoming (Harmonic) and as they become overcaring or smothering in order to get that attention from others (stress point). Their response to change translates their need for attention into being dramatic and prone to claiming they are misunderstood.

In contrast, Fours at high emotional health levels recognise that they truly are unique and special and bring this to their

4

everyday life. They use their many special talents and the way they view the world to come up with distinctive and innovative ideas and ways of doing things. They also help others to feel more deeply through creative and supportive approaches to expression.

As a Four aiming to move up the emotional health levels, you must learn to take the energy of the heart and your deep emotional intuition and integrate this with objectivity, so that you can find an equilibrium between your heart and mind. You must learn to find your sense of self-worth without comparing yourself to others, and learn to turn your focus to others as much as yourself.

Some of the actions you can take include:

- Don't equate depth with contribution – for yourself or others.

- Master pragmatic information and hard facts as a springboard for intuition and innovation.

- Be willing to negotiate and compromise without feeling that your integrity has been violated.

- Learn to name your feelings rather than being them – convey them rather than acting them out.

- Cultivate perspective to help you 'zoom out' and see context when you're overwhelmed.

- Don't take everything so personally – people act from their own interpretations of life. It's not all about you.

4

Strengthening your connection to type 4, as a non-Four

To strengthen this area if you don't have a strong connection to it you need to experience and appreciate the creativity you already have and use in your daily life. You can start by reflecting on and identifying what is unique and special about you. Aim to come up with at least 20 characteristics (on paper) that reflect this. You could also get feedback from others on what you currently do well (even if it does not sound creative to you) and acknowledging the effect and impact these things have on others.

Learn to value the difference you see around you and in others, be curious when you hear a different perspective or idea and look for the beauty in this. Notice the beauty all around you, as if you were seeing it for the first time, and truly appreciate the wonders of the world.

Type 5 psychological development guide

'I remain informed and objective.'

5

If we summarise what we know so far about type 5 it looks like this:

Gift	The gift of Fives is the ability to understand meaning and connection and thereby achieve genuine insight and grounded wisdom.
Basic fear	Being incompetent, useless and incapable.
Coping strategy	Collecting and analysing information to build their knowledge and capability.
Centre of intelligence	Head
Primary need	Security
Hornevian group*	Withdraw
Harmonic group†	Competent
Stress point	Type 7 (visionary to scattered)
Secure point	Type 8 (empowering to controlling)
Silent question	'What more do I need to know?'

* how they try to get their primary need met
† response to not having primary need met

The Five's instinctual variant – self-preservation, social or sexual (which is independent of their type or the other factors listed above) – further affects their personality, as it does for all types.

The Five's level of emotional health will also affect their behaviours and their responses to situations in which they find themselves.

Improving emotional health for the Five

Let's now look at what this means in terms of the Five who wants to increase their level of emotional health.

The Five at an average level of emotional health tends to specialise: they focus on a small number of areas in order to give themselves the best chance of gaining mastery and feeling competent. Their knowledge brings security. Their brains rarely switch off. 'I continuously think about and ponder other possibilities and ideas.' They can be, or at least appear, detached from others, sometimes even disinterested or dismissive.

You can see in behaviours such as these, elements of withdrawing in order to meet their primary need for security (Hornevian), moving deeper into data and information when they don't feel secure (Harmonic) and as they become more scattered with the endless possibilities the information brings (stress point). Their response to change translates their need for security into getting more and more information so they can work through it.

At high emotional health levels, Fives recognise when they have enough knowledge to participate in the world and share their insights and learning. They are wise, independent and clear and are not easily pulled into conventional ways of thinking. They genuinely understand meaning and real connection and deeply engage with others in exploring what is possible and how this can be achieved.

To move up the emotional health levels as a Five, you must learn to engage emotionally in real time rather than automatically disengaging from your emotional responses in order to remain 'competent' in the situation. You also need to practise being a central part of events, interpersonal interactions and organisations, rather than staying on the periphery.

In group situations you will often bring a high degree of autonomy, working alongside, as opposed to 'with', capable and efficient team members. However, you also need to be able to increase your ability to work in a more collaborative way when the work truly requires this.

Some of the actions you can take include:

- When communicating, watch for cues that your audience is bored or put off by your high (some might think excessive) level of knowledge.

- Practise taking the risk to express your position. Don't always play it safe or hide. Ask for more time if you need it before you say what's on your mind.

5

- Listen carefully – curb your habit of thinking while others are talking.

- Accept that work is collaborative – align with a few key people.

- Don't discount the human factor – people are emotional and you need to work with that.

- Let others know when you're open – and when you're not – to interactions, conversations and dialogue. Push yourself to be more open than not.

Strengthening your connection to type 5, as a non-Five

To strengthen this area if you don't have a strong connection to it, you need to develop a curiosity about how things work. Practise asking the question 'Why is it so?' on a frequent basis. It is about exploring a number of ideas and perspectives related to a topic and finding the connections and common themes and the links between these.

You could start by choosing a topic that has always interested you and begin to learn about it with some online searching, what you can find to read, what others who are in the subject field may know and through what presentations are available. Remember that it is always good to share your knowledge of the subject and what you are learning with someone else.

Type 6 psychological development guide

'I become more and more prepared.'

6

If we summarise what we know so far about type 6 it looks like this:

Gift	The gift of Sixes is the ability to actively support and steadfastly commit to people, groups and causes, ensuring their ongoing safety and security.
Basic fear	Having no support and guidance.
Coping strategy	Vigilantly noticing potential hazards, preparing for worst possible outcomes and guarding against the dangers of the world (including people).
Centre of intelligence	Head
Primary need	Security
Hornevian group*	Earn
Harmonic group†	Emotionally real/reactive
Stress point	Type 3 (achieving to opportunistic)
Secure point	Type 9 (inclusive to avoiding)
Silent question	'Am I going to be okay here?'

* how they try to get their primary need met
† response to not having primary need met

6

Once again, the Six's instinctual variant – self-preservation, social or sexual (which is independent of their type or the other factors listed above) – further affects their personality, as it does for all types.

The Six's level of emotional health will also affect their behaviours and their responses to situations in which they find themselves.

Improving emotional health for the Six

Let's now look at what this means in terms of the Six who wants to increase their level of emotional health.

We know that Sixes with an average level of emotional health are prone to being worried, indecisive and doubting. 'I am sceptical and continually question everything, which results in constant uncertainty.' They will often overthink situations; they will work hard to ensure all the options have been covered, but then still find themselves unable to make up their mind and reacting to the environment they are in. They can be strong in justifying and defending the status quo.

You can see in behaviours such as these, elements of doing what is right and what is expected in order to meet their primary need for security (Hornevian), becoming emotionally real/reactive when they believe they have no support and feel unsafe (Harmonic) and as they shift into working to get to a solution without knowing

6

what it takes to get there (stress point). Their response to change translates their need for security into getting constantly evaluating what is happening and trying to find ways to stay safe.

Sixes at high emotional health levels recognise problems and potential solutions to them, bringing foresight and strong organisational ability to achieve the right result. As a consequence, they create stability and security in their own world as well as for others. They bring a cooperative spirit that both engages and enables others.

As a Six, moving up the emotional health levels requires that you learn to not allow fear and inconstancy to have power and authority over you. You need to trust and be courageous; you must learn to trust yourself and not be misled by false authorities. You must also learn to stay on the path you have committed to, maintaining clear, steadfast movement forward.

Some of the actions you can take include:

- Don't be afraid to play the devil's advocate, but make sure you do it consciously to help, not reactively out of fear.

- Look for solutions to the problems you see.

- Learn to give compliments, express thanks and appreciate what's going well.

- Develop your own inner authority or gut instinct, which you can trust.

6

- Practise the process of trusting – notice what actions and evidence allow you to trust others.

- Use the word 'and' rather than 'but'.

- Remember all the times when you've felt the fear and done it anyway.

Strengthening your connection to type 6, as a non-Six

To strengthen this area if you don't have a strong connection to it, you need to develop your awareness of those things around you that could go wrong, along with identifying potential solutions to these issues. This means you will have to ask yourself what could go wrong and what would happen if it did. You will need to consciously think about this. It is very much a case of being prepared for those bigger problems that might come along and having a plan to deal with them.

Type 7 psychological development guide

'I look for the next possibility.'

If we summarise what we know so far about type 7 it looks like this:

Gift	The gift of Sevens is the ability to envision what is possible and inspire others through this.
Basic fear	Being deprived and trapped in emotional pain.
Coping strategy	Noticing options and opportunities and planning for the next pleasurable experience.
Centre of intelligence	Head
Primary need	Security
Hornevian group*	Assert
Harmonic group†	Positive outlook
Stress point	Type 1 (idealistic to perfectionistic)
Secure point	Type 5 (wise to isolated)
Silent question	'How do I move on/get out of here?'

* how they try to get their primary need met
† response to not having primary need met

7

As with the other types, the Seven's instinctual variant – self-preservation, social or sexual (which is independent of their type or the other factors listed above) – further affects their personality, as it does for all types.

The Seven's level of emotional health will also affect their behaviour and their responses to situations in which they find themselves.

Improving emotional health for the Seven

Let's now look at what this means in terms of Seven who wants to increase their level of emotional health.

Sevens of an average level of emotional health tend to be rebellious and irreverent. 'I am flippant and dismissive of rules and boundaries as I don't like to be limited.' They can turn almost anything into a joke as their way of dealing with anxieties and problems. They also have a tendency to be hyperactive and easily bored with mundane tasks, always looking for something new.

You can see in behaviours such as these some elements of being overly proactive in pursuit of their primary need for security (Hornevian), remaining upbeat and positive even if that is not really what they are experiencing (Harmonic) and as they shift into trying to create a semblance of order in the chaos they are experiencing (stress point). Their response to change translates their need for security into looking for a way to quickly share what to do to get out of it and move on.

Sevens at high emotional health levels recognise that all of life's experiences – positive and otherwise – contribute to their ongoing development and appreciation of the world around them. They assimilate experiences in depth, making them deeply grateful for what they have. They bring visionary thinking to change that inspires and engages others.

To move up the emotional health levels as a Seven, you must learn to focus mentally, emotionally and physically at will. You need to learn to connect to your heart, really take things in, value quality over quantity, and feel genuine and consistent empathy for others. You must learn to move into your depths, which is to experience both your pain and your pleasure, be willing to really feel your disappointment but also your joy, and to allow these feelings to sink in so that you can appreciate the satisfaction that comes from savouring the depths.

Some of the actions you can take include:

- Practise under-promising. Be more realistic and work to anticipate problems before they arise.

- Take small practical steps to actualise your vision.

- Learn to make choices: which ideas to share, which strategy to pursue, which party to attend.

- Be aware of your tendency to rationalise, trivialise or explain away. Taking responsibility is not the same as taking blame.

7

- Listen for and be more careful of others' feelings. They are not the bottomless pit of darkness that you fear.

- Finish what you start. Get some help with organisation and prioritisation and use your energy, optimism and sense of fun to help those working with you to coalesce.

Strengthening your connection to type 7, as a non-Seven

To strengthen this area if you don't have a strong connection to it, you need to experience the world of possibilities and opportunities, embracing the spontaneity that comes with the unexpected and recognising the joy and happiness inherent in these experiences.

You can start with exploring a situation or problem through the 'lens' of positive outlook, looking at what is possible and what the opportunities are, rather than beginning with the problems or issues. You can bring your knowledge and experience to the situation in a way that enables people to move forward as they see the possibilities.

Look for opportunities to step in and try new experiences simply to find out what they are like. Appreciate the excitement and joy of doing something new and the learning this creates.

The imbalance of the centres

Earlier in this book we introduced the concept of 'whole body thinking' and 'presence', and we described how those who achieve the highest emotional health level are able to live in presence at all times by achieving a balance of the body, heart and head centres. This balance extends to the Enneagram types: someone with the highest level of emotional health has access to all nine Enneagram types. They are no longer influenced by the basic fear of their primary Enneagram type; they no longer need to resort to the coping strategies of that type.

However, we know that people at this level are rare. As emotional health decreases to levels more typical in the wider population, we find that a 'shock point' occurs as we move from level 3 to level 4. At this point we find that one of our three centres starts to become 'distorted', the specific centre depending on our primary Enneagram type.

We refer to the emergence and existence of this distortion as an 'imbalance' of the centres (Figure 25). An interactive loop develops between this centre and one of our remaining centres that is often self-perpetuating. The other centre outside this loop is one we can

Figure 25: The imbalance of the centres

trust and it can play an important part in regaining balance. At level 4 we are usually aware of this other centre, though at level 5 we may not take any notice of it. (This interplay between the centres will become clearer when we discuss this in the context of the individual Enneagram types below.)

If we are unfortunate enough to fall to the lower emotional health levels, we encounter another shock point as we move from level 6 to level 7. Here the other centre becomes distorted as well, leaving only one centre as the one we trust and operate out of.

Understanding the imbalances of the centres gives us insight into the development path we need to take in order to increase our emotional health. It is a reminder that increasing our emotional health is not just a cognitive process and that presence comes about through the integration of the three centres.

We'll now look at the imbalance of the centres for each Enneagram type. There are a number of groupings that help us understand more about the imbalance and its impact. It is also easier to understand when we look at the three centres as the doing centre (body), feeling centre (heart) and thinking centre (head).

The Hornevian groups provide us with the initial framework for understanding the imbalance of the centres and for identifying appropriate development strategies, so we will use these groups in the following discussion.

The 'assertive' types: types 8, 7 and 3

The 'assertive' Hornevian group of Enneagram types – 8, 7 and 3 – are similar in that the two centres that form an interactive loop as we move from level 3 to level 4 are the thinking (head) centre and the doing (body) centre. One of these centres becomes distorted, the level of distortion increasing as we move down the emotional health levels to level 6.

Type 8

While type 8 lives in the doing centre, the first centre to become distorted as an Eight moves from level 3 to level 4 is the thinking centre. What follows is the creation of a doing–thinking interactive loop (Figure 26).

At emotional health level 4, Eights prefer to 'do' while engaging the thinking centre as part of the doing. They know what needs to be done, however they are conscious that they should think before acting, even though that is not their 'natural' inclination. At emotional health level 5, the thinking centre is more distorted so while the Eight will still want to 'do' first, thinking occurs simultaneously. This is

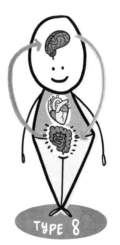

Figure 26: Type 8 doing–thinking loop

characterised by a habit of fixing things on the run. They know what needs to be done, take action, then fix any issues as they come up. At emotional health level 6 the thinking centre is even more distorted, to the point that there is almost no conscious connection to it. At this level the Eight 'does' (acts) first and any thinking only happens afterwards, often after having already created an issue or problem due to not thinking things through in the first place.

To summarise, at level 4 Eights think (briefly) before they act; at level 5 they think while they act; and at level 6 they think after they act. During all of this the centre outside the doing–thinking loop – the feeling (heart) centre – is free to be accessed and trusted should the Eight choose to do so. Accessing this centre helps the Eight to connect into their feelings and really experience all of life through an open heart. This helps the Eight out of the loop, helping them to also access the logic and clarity of the thinking centre, which in turn will enable them to move towards a balance of the centres.

If the Eight drops from emotional health level 6 to level 7, then the feeling centre also becomes distorted, leaving a mess of multiple interactive loops between the doing and thinking and doing and feeling centres. Only the doing centre remains trusted.

Type 7

Type 7 lives in the thinking centre; however, the first centre to become distorted for this type is the doing centre; the interactive loop that is created is a thinking–doing loop (Figure 27).

At emotional health level 4, Sevens prefer the thinking centre. They are quick to engage the doing centre to enact their many thoughts and ideas. They think about what outcomes are needed and briefly consider what needs to be done (and whether it should be done) to get those outcomes. They then move quickly to action. At emotional health level 5, the Seven's doing centre is more distorted so their thinking–doing

Figure 27: Type 7 thinking–doing loop

loop is more simultaneous. There is only a small pause between thinking and action as they adapt to new thoughts as they (constantly) arise. There is not much time to ponder whether or not a thought should be enacted. At emotional health level 6, with their doing centre even more distorted, Sevens tend to think and 'do' in one step, without comprehending the impact and/or issues created by acting on every thought without pause. They can often get side-tracked by new thoughts along the way, which soon turn into new actions. This is all very stimulating to the Seven, though it can leave behind those they are working with or leading.

In summary, at level 4 the Seven prefers to act out every idea but thinks (briefly) before doing so; at level 5 they think and act simultaneously, adapting to new thoughts as they arise; and at level 6 there is little in the way of a 'filter' between thought and action. During all of this the centre outside the thinking–doing loop, the feeling centre, is free and can be accessed and trusted much as it can for the Eight. Accessing this centre helps the Seven to connect into their feelings and really experience life through an open heart. This helps the Seven out of the loop, which allows them to also access the groundedness of the doing (body) centre and move towards a balance of the centres.

If the Seven drops from emotional health level 6 to level 7 then they lose touch with the feeling centre just as the Eight does. In the Seven's case this leaves the thinking centre as their only trusted centre.

Type 3

Type 3 lives in the feeling centre; however, as the Three moves through the shock point between emotional health levels 3 and 4, they start to become segregated from this centre. Note that this is different to Sevens and Eights. An interactive loop in this case does not include the primary centre, but rather forms between the other two centres. In practice this means that Threes start to keep their emotions (their feeling centre) out of the way, concentrating instead on being efficient and effective. Allowing emotions in will start to affect their performance. Of the two 'non-primary' centres, one will be strong for them while the other tends to be distorted. The loop that is created is either a thinking–doing interactive loop or a doing–thinking interactive loop (Figure 28), depending on which centre is the stronger. In other words, the

Figure 28: Type 3 thinking–doing/ doing–thinking loop

Three's interactive loops at emotional health levels 4, 5 and 6 can look like those characterised by either the type 8 doing–thinking loop or the type 7 thinking–doing loop. At the same time, the characteristics of the type 3 with average emotional health continue to manifest in these interactive loops. Threes maintain the habit of looking to please others, consistent with the drive of their primary feeling centre and the need for attention and/or validation. Finding ways to re-integrate that centre will assist with achieving balance of the three centres.

Threes will often talk about how their feelings get in the way of their performing and how they can get stuck in those feelings. At level 4, they often refer to two modes of being: 'performance mode', which is connected to the thinking–doing or doing–thinking loops, and 'feeling mode', where they access the segregating feeling centre and end up caught in how they feel. The performance mode is driven by the doing–thinking or thinking–doing loop that moves them to action.

If the Three drops from emotional health level 6 to level 7, they lose touch with the distorted centre and identify only with the last remaining centre (either thinking or doing).

Development activities for the assertive types: connecting with the heart (feeling) centre

If you identify with one of the above types, connecting with your heart centre will enable you to overcome the interactive loop that occurs between the other two centres. The following activities will help you move toward integration of the three centres – essential to improving your level of emotional health.

- Get in touch with your heart by expressing your feelings in words. Write them down or talk with someone about them.

- Slow down your pace and really experience your life. Take time to notice your feelings. 'Smell the roses', walk barefoot in the sand, enjoy your family. Have some playtime.

- Open up your heart by doing something for someone else. Do something you wouldn't normally do, just because it will make someone else happy. Do this without expecting anything in return. Notice how you feel as a result.

- Go somewhere where you can connect to your heart with what is going on around you, for example with family, with music, engaging in a social cause.

- Listen/play music that arouses your heart and notice the feelings this generates.

- Build the link between feelings and performance, understanding the emotions that sit underneath.

- Be authentic by connecting into your heart and opening up to your feelings and vulnerabilities.

Each of the Enneagram types can have a behaviour that acts as a 'block' to their development. Eights might not like the suggested development path and want to do it their own way; Sevens often can't avoid thinking about the next thing rather than staying focused on what is at hand; Threes might constantly ask, 'Am I doing it right, best or beautifully?' It is good to observe your responses or reactions to the above suggestions and take notice of those that make you feel the most uncomfortable. What are you telling yourself about why you cannot do this?

The 'withdrawing' types: types 4, 5 and 9

The 'withdrawing' Hornevian group of Enneagram, types 4, 5 and 9, are similar in that the two centres that form an interactive loop as we move from level 3 to level 4 are the thinking (head) centre and the feeling (heart) centre. One of these centres becomes distorted at that point, the level of distortion increasing as we move down the emotional health levels.

Type 4

Fours live in the feeling centre. The first centre to become distorted for them is the thinking centre, and this leads to the creation of a feeling–thinking loop (Figure 29).

At emotional health level 4, Fours prefer the feeling centre. They want to feel deeply, but they also engage with their thinking centre to increase their imagination and creativity. Although the thinking centre is somewhat distorted, Fours allow that centre to play a role in their responses because they understand the benefits. At emotional health level 5, the thinking centre is more distorted, causing Fours to

Figure 29: Type 4 feeling–thinking loop

immerse themselves in their feelings while simultaneously engaging their thinking. This tight feeling–thinking loop causes a ramping up of the intensity of their feelings. At emotional health level 6, the thinking centre is further distorted. Fours become caught up in their own feelings; any thinking they are doing is almost impossible to distinguish from those feelings and may only occur in retrospect. At this level they tend to withdraw to protect themselves and live in their own imaginary world.

To summarise, at level 4 the Enneagram type 4 is guided by their feelings, but their responses are moderated by their thinking; at level 5 their thinking has less impact, as it takes place in conjunction with their feeling; and at level 6 they feel first and only think afterwards. During all of this the centre outside the feeling–thinking loop – the doing (body) centre – is free to be trusted and accessed should they choose to do so. Accessing this centre helps the Four to connect into the groundedness and knowing of that centre. This helps the Four out of the loop, which allows them to also access the logic, clarity and spaciousness of the thinking centre and move towards a balance of the centres.

If the Four drops from emotional health level 6 to level 7, the doing centre also becomes distorted, leaving multiple interactive loops between the feeling and thinking centres and the feeling and doing centres. Only the feeling centre remains trusted.

Type 5

While Fives live in the thinking centre, the first centre to become distorted for them is the feeling centre, leading to a thinking–feeling loop (Figure 30).

At emotional health level 4, Fives prefer to think while also engaging the feeling centre to increase their love for ideas. This passion for ideas has them seeking to understand how things work and the interconnections between them. They are comfortable displaying this love of ideas to others, while they also allow their feelings to keep a check on their (potentially endless) curiosity. At emotional health level 5, the Five's

Figure 30: Type 5 thinking–feeling loop

feeling centre is more distorted and less capable of tempering the deep desire to think, to explore new ideas, to understand. Emotions (feelings) are invested in their thinking but potentially in a less constructive and more self-indulgent way. At emotional health level 6, the Five's thinking and feeling become difficult to distinguish. Their internal emotions no longer act as a check on their thinking, but rather drive it as their imagination and curiosity take them down multiple paths of enquiry before they opt to focus ever more deeply into one thing. They tend to withdraw into their own world, where they can continue to explore uninterrupted.

To summarise, at level 4 the Enneagram type 5 is driven by their thinking and their emotional attachment to that, but their feelings also provide a check; at level 5 their feelings become more internal and their thinking can become more self-indulgent; at level 6 their curiosity can run away unchecked. During all of this the Five's doing (body) centre, which is outside the thinking–feeling loop, is free to be accessed and trusted. Accessing this centre helps the Five to connect into the groundedness and knowing of that centre. This helps the Five out of the loop, which allows them to also access the heart centre, connecting into all of their feelings and really experiencing all of life. This in turn enables them to move towards a balance of the centres.

If the Five drops from emotional health level 6 to level 7, the doing centre also becomes distorted, as with type 4, leaving the thinking centre as the only centre the Five can trust.

Type 9

Nines live in the doing centre; however, as Nines move through the shock point between emotional health levels 3 and 4 they start to become segregated from that centre. Of the other two centres – thinking and feeling – one of them will be strong while the other will tend to be distorted. This leads to the creation of either a thinking–feeling loop or a feeling–thinking loop (Figure 31).

In other words, Nines' interactive loops, at an average level of emotional health (level 4, 5 or 6) look like those characterised by either a type 4 feeling–thinking loop or a type 5 thinking–feeling loop. At the same time, the characteristics of the Nine with average emotional health continue to manifest in these interactive loops, with a strong internal desire to maintain their autonomy. In both cases also, the doing centre

Figure 31: Type 9 thinking–feeling/ feeling–thinking loop

remains free but segregated from the other two centres. Finding ways to re-integrate that centre will assist with achieving balance of the three centres.

Nines will often talk about feeling disconnected within themselves. This creates an uneasy and uncomfortable feeling within that they look to minimise by withdrawing inwards and avoiding situations they perceive will make it worse. At level 4 they often refer to two modes of being: 'daydream mode', which is connected to the feeling–thinking or thinking–feeling loops, and 'instinct mode', where they access the segregating doing centre. Of these, the 'active' mode is determined by which centre they are most strongly connected to at that point in time.

If the Nine drops from emotional health level 6 to level 7, the doing centre becomes even more segregated and they lose touch with it altogether. Part of the reason for this segregation is as a protection mechanism to distance themselves from the rising anger that manifests from this centre in the lower emotional health levels. The anger can feel so strong that it often frightens them.

Development activities for the withdrawing types: connecting with the body (doing) centre

If you identify with one of the above types, connecting with your body centre will enable you to overcome the interactive loop that occurs between the other two centres. The following activities will help you move toward integration of the three centres – essential to improving your level of emotional health.

- Engage in the body centre by doing: jump in and do what needs to be done. Pick up the rubbish, weed the garden, clean your house, wash the car.

- Move your body. Feel your body. Dance, walk, do Tai Chi, learn a martial art, go to dance classes. Swim and feel the water on your skin. Breathe.

- Connect to your body. If you meditate, make it an active form, such as walking meditation. Play active sports.

- You need kinesthetic exercise – exercise that engages the

body in activity. This will connect you to your body centre and ground you.

As previously mentioned, each of the Enneagram types can have a behaviour that acts as a 'block' to their development. Fives might want to get more information about the suggestions as they haven't researched this themselves. Fours might see what is suggested as 'mundane' or 'ordinary'. Nines might hesitate to actively engage as it is 'too much, too soon'. It is good to observe your responses or reactions to the above suggestions and take notice of those that make you feel the most uncomfortable. What are you telling yourself about why you cannot do this?

The 'earning' types: types 1, 2 and 6

The 'earning' Hornevian group of Enneagram types – 1, 2 and 6 – are similar in that the two centres that form an interactive loop at the first shock point of level 3 to level 4 are the feeling (heart) centre and the doing (body) centre. Again, one of these centres becomes distorted at that point, with the level of distortion increasing as a person moves further down the emotional health levels.

Type 1

While Ones live in the doing centre, the first centre to become distorted for them is the feeling centre, leading to the creation of a doing–feeling loop (Figure 32).

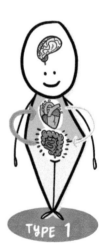

At emotional health level 4, Ones prefer to engage the feeling centre in order to get things done. It is often their passion for getting things done in the right way that moves them to action. They are comfortable sharing their idealistic views about the path that needs to be followed. At emotional health level 5, the feeling centre is more distorted. Ones 'do' while simultaneously immersing themselves in their feelings, bringing a sense of

Figure 32: Type 1 doing–feeling loop

harsh judgement on themselves and others about whether things have been done well enough. They can be quick to criticise themselves or others about what needs to be done to improve. At emotional health level 6, Ones just 'do' first, then 'feel' afterwards. Their doing and feeling become mixed and confused and they often become resentful, perfectionistic and opinionated. They will often not listen to others as they believe that what they are doing is right. If no one is taking any notice of what they are saying, their anger can show up as seething frustration.

In summary, at level 4 the One uses their feelings to help them get things done; at level 5 their feelings cause them to become more judgemental as they 'do'; and at level 6 their feelings confuse the way they judge their actions (and those of others). During all of this their thinking centre, which is outside the doing–feeling loop, is free. Accessing the logic, clarity and spaciousness of this centre can help the One out of the loop and move them towards balance of the centres. It can also allow them to access an open heart, where they can connect into all their feelings and really experience all of life.

If the One drops from emotional health level 6 to level 7 then the thinking centre shuts down. The doing (body) centre remains their only trusted centre.

Type 2

Twos live in the feeling centre. The first centre to become distorted for them is the doing centre, creating a feeling–doing loop (Figure 33).

At emotional health level 4, they prefer to feel while engaging the doing (body) centre. They aim to please people by their actions so that they will be liked and loved; however, their body centre keeps a check on this so that they don't drown others in their 'good deeds'. At emotional health level 5, their doing centre is more distorted. They feel and simultaneously 'do'. In practice this means they do things for others in order to be loved by them. Loving someone now means doing something for them. At emotional health level 6 the doing centre is further distorted. They feel and 'do' together; they are expressing their feelings through their actions. They ignore their own needs and focus wholly on taking care of others to gain their love; the distortion of their feelings prevents them from being attuned to when their actions move from being helpful to being intrusive.

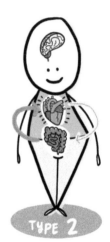

Figure 33: Type 2 feeling–doing loop

In summary, at level 4 the Two's desire to help is inspired by, but also kept in check by, their feelings; at level 5 they see 'doing' as the best way of expressing their feelings; and at level 6 doing and feeling are one, which can lead to 'excessive' expressions of love through action. As with Ones, during all of this their thinking centre is free. Accessing this centre helps the Two to connect into grounded logic, clarity and spaciousness. This helps the Two out of the loop and allows them to access the groundedness and knowing of the doing centre, moving them towards a balance of the centres.

If the Two drops from emotional health level 6 to level 7 then the thinking centre becomes distorted, along with the already distorted doing centre. The feeling centre remains their only trusted centre.

Type 6

Sixes live in the thinking centre, however as they move through the shock point of level 3 to level 4, they start to become segregated from that centre. One of the other two centres will be strong for them, while the other tends to be distorted. The result is the creation of either a doing–feeling loop or a feeling–doing loop (Figure 34).

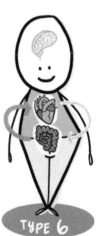

Figure 34: Type 6 doing–feeling/ feeling/loop

At an average level of emotional health (level 4, 5 or 6) these loops look like those characterised by either the One's doing–feeling loop or the Two's feeling–doing loop. At the same time, the characteristics of the type 6 with average emotional health continue to manifest, such as identifying risks in their environment and establishing support from others. In both cases the head centre remains free but segregated from both other centres. Finding ways to re-integrate that centre will assist with achieving balance of the three centres.

Sixes will often talk about having unclear thinking and how their thinking can go in circles, creating a lot of self-doubt. At level 4, they often refer to two modes of being: the 'dutiful mode', which is connected to the feeling–doing or doing–feeling loops, and the 'thinking mode', where they access the segregated thinking centre, with the resultant circular thinking. In the 'dutiful mode', where the doing and feeling centres drive their action, we see the earning characteristic come through.

As the Six moves down the emotional health levels the segregation of their thinking centre increases. If they drop from emotional health level 6 to level 7 then the thinking centre becomes even more segregated and they lose touch with it altogether. They are left identifying with only their original strong centre – either the doing or feeling centre.

Development activities for the earning types: connecting with the head (thinking) centre

If you identify with one of the above types, connecting with your head centre will enable you to overcome the interactive loop that occurs between the other two centres. The following activities will help you move toward integration of the three centres – essential to improving your level of emotional health.

- Use mindfulness meditation, focusing on your breathing. Watch where your thoughts go and keep bringing them back to the present.

- Observe yourself when you're with other people. Notice the judgements you make about them. Also notice how you accommodate yourself for others and lose your own point of view.

- Notice the language you use and how often you use conditional words like 'maybe', 'sort of', 'probably', 'likely', 'it depends'. Can you make up your own mind?

- Talk through issues and problems to gain clarity.

- Brief exercise can provide a break that will enable you to engage your thinking centre and bring logic and clarity. Enabling your thinking centre often involves being grounded, which is achieved in our body through exercise.

Each of the Enneagram types can have a behaviour that acts as a 'block' to their development. Ones might want to avoid talking through issues as they believe they should already have the answer; Twos might feel they are being selfish in taking time for themselves to meditate; Sixes might avoid making up their mind, as they can always find another reason not to. It is good to watch your responses or reactions to the above suggestions and take notice of those that make you feel the most uncomfortable. What are you telling yourself about why you cannot do this?

Somatic development
Paths to building emotional health

At the start of Part 3 we noted that there are two pathways of development in the pursuit of moving up the emotional health levels: the psychological and the somatic, with the imbalance of the centres providing a connection between the two. Having now looked at the psychological pathway and the imbalance of the centres, let's investigate the somatic practices – practices that will actively engage your body, and through that help you achieve engagement of all three centres.

In this section we will introduce you to a range of somatic practices that maximise the use of our physical body in accessing our senses, emotions, perceptions, thoughts and actions and, in doing so enable us to access more of our 'less preferred' centres, which in turn helps us to create new pathways and patterns of behaviour and response. This section builds on what has been covered in Part 3 so far, in particular the imbalance of the centres. First, we will offer some general suggestions and then we will go into specific somatic practices relevant to each Enneagram type.

Breaking out of the patterns we get caught in

Bringing our thoughts, feelings and senses into our 'conscious now' is one of the greatest challenges we face. The neural pathways that maintain our current patterns of thinking and behaviour have been built over a long time – since childhood for most of us. We are drawn to continue these patterns, and it is very difficult to stop doing something we are very used to doing, even if we would prefer not to. When we recognise aspects of ourselves that we want to change, regardless of which centre or centres they are coming from, it takes time and persistence to make those changes.

The first step toward making a change is to identify how we would prefer to think or feel, or what we want to do differently when a particular 'trigger' arrives. This is where the 'inner observer' described on page 17 is so important. When we can learn to catch ourselves in our automatic reactions – in the 'magic quarter second' – and acknowledge the return of 'established' patterns, we can choose a new and preferred thought, feeling or action. When we do this, we start to build a new neural pathway for how we would like to be. The more we use this new pathway, the stronger it becomes and the weaker our old pathways become at the same time.

Somatic practices enable us to embed these new pathways. They can provide a very strong link between our physical movement and our thinking and feeling. Understanding this connection and the practice of 'whole body' listening is a critical facet in the development of our emotional health.

Thinking with your 'whole body'

We have already discussed the centres of intelligence and 'whole body thinking' at some length, and given that, it is sufficient at this point to restate that integrating and bringing full attention to all three centres of intelligence – the body, heart and head – enables us to increase our range of behavioural freedom and emotional health. It also provides us with the opportunity to be more 'in the moment' than not, and furthers our ability to be 'in the zone' or 'in the flow' – that is, in 'presence'. All of this lies at the core of moving up the emotional health levels.

There are a great many somatic practices and techniques you can draw on to improve your ability to integrate the three centres for yourself. Eastern traditions have included this focus for thousands of years through meditation, yoga, martial arts, tai chi, qigong and so on. However, you can also do things as simple as removing your shoes and walking quietly along a beach; sitting under a tree in a park or forest and noticing the sounds around you; taking in an amazing view at the top of a hill or mountain; watching dolphins leaping and cavorting alongside a boat; playing in the sun with your children or pet; lying on the grass, closing your eyes and noticing the smells. All of these and similar activities can increase the integration of the centres for you.

Even when all of these seem like remote possibilities, when the world of work is right in front of you and options for being present are less than obvious, there are still practices you can adopt to engage all three centres. For instance, in the work environment you may notice that you are over-analysing something, have too many ideas or suggestions to consider or are relying on others to provide their thoughts and ideas instead of coming up with your own. All of these are indicators that you may be out of touch with your body centre. A simple method to bring your focus back to your body is to sit upright on a chair with both feet on the floor, your hands flat on your knees and your eyes closed (or looking at the floor and 'blurring' your focus). Press your hands gently on your knees for 30 seconds so that you can feel the pressure. Notice how the mind moves to where the pressure is and what happens to your thoughts as a result. Another good way to stay connected with the body centre and encourage a quiet mind is through regular exercise. Simply taking a 15-minute walk every lunchtime is a good start.

Two other common situations you may find yourself in at work are feeling very judgemental about another person in a meeting or having difficulty understanding where someone is coming from in terms of how they are expressing themselves. These are both signs that you may be out of touch with your heart centre. To reconnect with your feelings and intuition and hold caring and compassion instead of judgement (without being too obvious), simply lean forward on your chair and rest an elbow on the table or desk, then place your hand on your chest over your heart as you look at the person or others in the room you are feeling disconnected from.

To maintain your connection to the heart centre outside work, try to create opportunities for social engagement. This is even easier when it involves an activity you are passionate about. For instance, if you love the outdoors then consider joining a walking club; if you enjoy music and singing then find a choir to get involved with.

Finally, if you find yourself struggling for awareness about or understanding of a situation, or you need to make sense of a large amount of information or data you are receiving, you may have lost connection with your head centre. An easy technique for remedying this at your desk involves putting your elbow on the table and cupping your chin in your hand. It's amazing how this simple 'clearing' activity can clarify your thoughts and provide fresh insight.

Interestingly, we have also found that connecting to the head centre often requires getting rid of the mental 'chatter' first. Starting the process of connection by using techniques and practices from the other two centres – taking a walk or playing a piece of music, for instance – brings a sense of calm, relaxation and clarity.

Time and practice will be your friends again when it comes to integrating your centres of intelligence. However, the good thing about the techniques described here is that they are mostly proactive and don't require your inner observer to 'catch the reaction'. Simply building practices that promote connection to all three centres into your daily or weekly routine will, over time, promote greater balance.

Having a clear intent

A question we (the authors) often ask when working with others on the path to increasing their emotional health is, 'How do you want to be or be seen?' Answers to this question typically invoke words like 'confident', 'inspiring' or 'engaging' – words that can completely change the way we present and work with others.

The aim of this question is to introduce the concept of 'intent'. Having a clear intent is about a state of mind – one that comes with sincere commitment. Central to having a clear intent is the notion of knowing how you want to be or be seen as opposed to what you want to do. Intent is about establishing a designated quality or behaviour, which in turn creates appropriate actions consistent with that quality or behaviour.

As an example, if we are co-facilitating a workshop, prior to the start we will often privately share an intent to be 'seamless'. We don't communicate this intent publicly with the workshop participants, yet often someone will come up to us during the day, unprompted, and comment on how seamlessly we work together – using that exact word. The same thing often happens when we share an intent to be 'collaborative'.

On a broader scale, it is intent that keeps our organisation on track, year after year. When we set up Global Leadership Foundation our intent was threefold: to be self-realised, collaborative and stewards for community (environment, social, local and global). This intent has constantly guided our decision making and presented opportunities that are in tune with how we want our organisation to be.

Introducing the notion of intent to your life is not difficult, and there are some simple and effective ways to begin.

When starting out, the best action to take is to state your intent each morning for the day ahead. Do this by choosing a word or words (usually no more than three) that describe the way you would like to be today. Prompt yourself by asking a question of intent like: 'How do I want to engage with others today?', 'How do I want to be as I meet new people today?' or 'How do I want to be in the meeting today?' Words like 'confident', 'inspiring', 'engaging', 'relaxed' or 'connected' will often appear in response to questions like this.

If your day is spent in your office – writing a report, for instance – your intent might be something like 'focused', 'calm' and 'clear'.

Of course, all these words are only suggestions and we will give some ideas for each of the Enneagram types in the next section. The trick in stating your intent is to keep it short: one to three words are preferable. Also, make sure you choose words that have 'real' meaning relating to the way you want to be and how others will experience you – not what you want to do. There is a difference.

When stating your intent, it must be verbalised. Your intent must 'leave your head'. A good way to do this is to tell someone else: your partner or a trusted work colleague. (Ideally in this case you will share each other's intents.) If you can't share your intent with someone else, send a voicemail to yourself. Or just say it out loud: dogs and cats can be good listeners. Other strategies are to write your intent on a piece of paper – any piece of paper – or to write it in a journal. Journals can be a good way of tracking your intent over time.

That said, don't actively review your intent. This point can be hard to comprehend for many who hold fast to the precept of 'You manage what you measure'. However, the point of stating an intent is not to constantly remind yourself of it during the day, nor to mechanistically review its success or otherwise at the end of the day. It is about embodying how you want to be. You'll know if you've been effective. Look for signs in others: the glint in the eye of a friend or someone you are working with, a newfound enthusiasm in one of your team or the time it takes to complete that report.

Like learning to operate above the line, all of this takes time and practice. It is important that you stick at it. Don't expect instant results and never expect specific results – 'If I act with confidence, I will get that deal'. Rather, get into the habit of stating your intent every day and, over time, you will start to notice the impact it is having.

We also like to take intent to a new level by embodying 'how we want to be' in our physical being, that is, 'putting ourselves in the experience'.

Let's start with a story to demonstrate what we mean. Imagine you are going to a special dinner. You have purchased a new outfit for this occasion and when you get dressed that evening you look in the mirror and go, 'Wow!' You look and feel like a million dollars. What happens to the way you are standing, to the way you walk, to your facial expressions? More than likely you stand tall. You are confident in the way you walk; your smile is radiant. During the evening people comment on how confident and great you look. This is not just about your new clothes – it is about your whole being. Your feelings – mainly confidence in this instance – are embodied in how you physically present.

The embodying of intent increases the strength of new neural pathways for the quality we are starting to create. The challenge is to identify how a quality you desire feels in your whole body and then to re-create that feeling.

It has to be said that for some people embodying their intent can be difficult. Many of us require support or coaching through the initial stages, either to help in identifying the right words for our intent and what the embodiment feels like, or to help us see success in terms of increased emotional health rather than more 'tangible' outcomes.

Specific somatic practices for Enneagram types

As we have identified, it takes time and practice for us to recognise and distinguish the three centres in action and to be able to effectively integrate them. The following guides will help you understand what to look for and recommend somatic practices for each of the Enneagram types to help you move from emotional health level 5 or 4 to level 3. As you read through these guides you may like to refer to the summary tables for the relevant types found between pages 139 and 174.

Type 8 somatic development guide

Connecting into the heart centre is a key to an Eight's development. Recall that the imbalance of the centres identified that Eights can get caught in a doing–thinking interactive loop, and that breaking that loop requires them to connect into the heart centre. Staying connected into the heart centre is a method for preventing the interactive loop from recurring. When this is achieved, Eights can fully access the thinking centre and all of its gifts through conscious practices.

As a first step, take a moment to connect with something or someone you love and *feel* that connection. Notice what you are feeling and allow this to permeate your whole body. Often placing an open hand over our heart speeds up this connection. Many people do this naturally in their communications so it is a very acceptable thing to do. Stay connected to what you are feeling and to your heart and notice the impact this has on how you now perceive what is going on around you. Eights know what this feels like when they move to their secure point of type 2, so often it is about recalling that embodied feeling and looking at how they can recreate it.

Balanced breathing is a quick way to balance the autonomic nervous system (responsible for control of the bodily functions not consciously directed, such as breathing, the heartbeat and digestive processes). It will also help you to connect your three centres together. Balanced breathing is achieved by taking a slow six-second breath in followed by six-second breath out, repeating this for at least three minutes. Six or even nine minutes may be needed if you've been through a disruptive period.

Eights can also be prone to reacting to situations, so simply taking a deep breath and exhaling before you say anything, or even counting to ten before reacting, can really make a difference.

It is also good to look for practices that are gentle in nature, or that do not require controlling. For example, try 'listening without knowing', where you listen intently to what someone is saying to you from a position of not knowing what they are going to say – as if they were speaking to you for the very first time. Another useful practice is 'allowing', in which you watch (instead of controlling) a course of action unfold through the engagement and participation of others while not interfering yourself. This may involve asking gentle questions using a coaching style while allowing others to lead the situation. Avoid allowing yourself to take over!

With the feeling centre connected, Eights will now find it easy to access the undistorted clarity of the thinking centre.

Good self-care is essential for everyone. Ensure you have beneficial sleep and nutrition and maintain regular exercise.

Having clear intent as a type 8

In creating the habit of having a clear intent, the following are some suggested words that can strengthen emotional health for the Eight; accepting, mentoring, empowering, enterprising, resolving, allowing.

Type 9 somatic development guide

Connecting into the body centre is a key to a Nine's development. The imbalance of the centres identified that Nines can get caught in either a feeling–thinking or thinking–feeling interactive loop while they remain segregated from their primary body centre. Ironically, breaking either of the loops requires them to connect into the body centre. Staying connected into the body centre is a method for preventing the interactive loops from recurring. When this is achieved, Nines can fully access the thinking and feeling centres and all of their gifts through conscious practices.

Balanced breathing is a quick way to balance the autonomic nervous system (responsible for control of the bodily functions not consciously directed, such as breathing, the heartbeat and digestive processes). It will also help you to connect your three centres together. Balanced breathing is achieved by taking a slow six-second breath in followed by a six-second breath out, repeating this for at least three minutes. Six or even nine minutes may be needed if you've been through a disruptive period.

Physical activity is the best way for the Nine to connect into their body centre. It helps them to become grounded and when this occurs they talk about feeling whole and connected. Going for a brisk walk of at least 20 minutes will start this happening. Climbing flights of stairs rather than using the lift or escalators whenever you can (e.g. when going to meetings) is a simple thing you can do at work. Other regular exercise such as cycling, gym workouts, aerobic exercise or even singing will also help. It is important to notice the impact of these activities and their effect on your becoming 'whole'.

Avoid the 'urge to merge' – the tendency to want to blend in. Step in and suggest what you would like at the outset. Suggest other alternatives. Notice how this is for you and what occurs. This all becomes easier if you are connected to your body centre.

With the doing centre connected, Nines will find it easy to access the undistorted clarity of the thinking centre and/or the passion of the feeling centre, depending on their preferred centre.

Good self-care is essential for everyone. Ensure you have beneficial sleep and nutrition and maintain regular exercise.

Having a clear intent as a type 9

In creating the habit of having a clear intent, the following are some suggested words that can strengthen emotional health for the Nine: resolute, congruent, harmonious, patient, inclusive, mediating.

Type 1 somatic development guide

Connecting into the head centre is a key to a One's development. The imbalance of the centres identified that Ones can get caught in a doing–feeling interactive loop and that breaking that loop requires them to connect into the head centre. Staying connected into the head centre is a method for preventing the interactive loop from recurring. When this is achieved, Ones can fully access the feeling centre and all of its gifts through conscious practices.

Balanced breathing is a quick way to balance the autonomic nervous system (responsible for control of the bodily functions not consciously directed, such as breathing, the heartbeat and digestive processes). It will also help you to connect your three centres together. Balanced breathing is achieved by taking a slow six-second breath in followed by a six-second breath out, repeating this for at least three minutes. Six or nine minutes will increase the effectiveness and give better results.

Walking outside in nature will help your mind and give clarity in your thinking. Dancing with freeform movements that are spontaneous and irregular, rather than structured and predictable, and cycling (in particular) appear to give Ones a clear mind and clarity.

Connecting into the head centre can sometimes be as simple as holding or resting your head in your hands, or simply putting your hands on your head. It is good to take notice of whether you already do this, or something similar, unconsciously. Try to bring these practices into your conscious thought.

Creating opportunities to be spontaneous and enjoying the pleasures of life also enable connection to the head centre. Some Ones find arranging a holiday that has an organised beginning (airfares and accommodation) and an organised ending (airfares) enables them to be spontaneous and fun loving in between arriving and departing.

Gardening is also a great way to accept what comes and goes, and that perfection lies in what is created naturally. Make the most of the environment and engage all of your senses – taste, sound, smell, touch and sight – as well as perceptions.

With the thinking centre connected, Ones find it easy to access the undistorted passion of the feeling centre.

Good self-care is essential for everyone. Ensure you have beneficial sleep and nutrition and maintain regular exercise.

Having a clear intent as a type 1

In creating the habit of having a clear intent, the following are some suggested words that can strengthen emotional health for the One: aligned, impartial, discerning, conscientious, ethical, principled.

Type 2 somatic development guide

Connecting into the head centre is a key to a Two's development. The imbalance of the centres identified that Twos can get caught in a feeling–doing interactive loop, and that breaking that loop requires them to connect into the head centre. They need to think before they do. Staying connected into the head centre is a method for preventing the interactive loop from recurring. When this is achieved, Twos can fully access the doing centre and all of its gifts through conscious practices.

Balanced breathing is a quick way to balance the autonomic nervous system (responsible for control of the bodily functions not consciously directed, such as breathing, the heartbeat and digestive processes). It will also help you to connect your three centres together. Balanced breathing is achieved by taking a slow six-second breath in followed by a six-second breath out, repeating this for at least three minutes. Six or nine minutes will increase the effectiveness and give better results.

Walking alone outside in nature and cycling (in particular) help clear the Two's mind and give clarity.

Connecting into the head centre can sometimes be as simple as holding or resting your head in your hands, or simply putting your hands on your head. It is good to take notice of whether you already do this, or something similar, unconsciously. Try to bring these practices into your conscious thought.

Making time for personal retreats that enable individual renewal is also important for the Two. This is all about finding time for 'self' and is best done alone rather than with others. In groups, the Two can get caught up looking after everyone else rather than themselves.

Gardening is a great way for Twos to focus on the process in the moment. Make the most of the environment and engage all of the senses – taste, sound, smell, touch and sight – as well as perceptions.

With the thinking centre connected, Twos find it easy to access the undistorted drive of the doing centre.

Good self-care is essential for everyone. Ensure you have beneficial sleep and nutrition and maintain regular exercise.

Having a clear intent as a type 2

In creating the habit of having a clear intent, the following are some suggested words that can strengthen emotional health for the Two: honouring, deeply caring, sensing, nurturing, generous, serving others.

Type 3 somatic development guide

Connecting into the heart is a key to a Three's development. The imbalance of the centres identified that Threes can get caught in either a thinking–doing or a doing–thinking interactive loop, while segregating from their primary heart centre. Ironically, breaking either of the loops requires them to connect into the heart centre. Staying connected into the heart centre is a method for preventing the interactive loops from recurring. When this is achieved, Threes can fully access the thinking or doing centre and all of its gifts through conscious practices.

As a first step, take a moment to connect into something or someone you love and *feel* that connection. Notice what you are feeling and allow this to permeate your whole body. Often placing an open hand over the heart speeds up this connection. Many people do this naturally in their communications so it is a very acceptable thing to do. Stay connected to this feeling and to your heart and also notice the impact this has on how you now perceive what is going on around you. Think of a time in the past when you have felt this way, recalling that embodied feeling and looking at how you can re-create it.

Balanced breathing is a quick way to balance the autonomic nervous system (responsible for control of the bodily functions not consciously directed, such as breathing, the heartbeat and digestive processes). It will also help you to connect your three centres together. Balanced breathing is achieved by taking a slow six-second breath in followed by a six-second breath out, repeating this for at least three minutes. Six or nine minutes will increase the effectiveness and give better results.

It is good to move from doing to being, appreciating the connections you have with others around you and the love others have for who you are as a person and not what you do or the status you hold. Seek to be modest and charitable, without wanting anything in return.

With the feeling centre now connected, Threes find it easy to access the undistorted drive of the doing centre and/or the clarity of the thinking centre.

Good self-care is essential for everyone. Ensure you have beneficial sleep and nutrition and maintain regular exercise.

Having a clear intent as a type 3

In creating the habit of having a clear intent, the following are some suggested words that can strengthen emotional health for the Three: gracious, admirable, self-assured, engaging, role model, ambitious.

Type 4 somatic development guide

Connecting into the body centre is a key to a Four's development. The imbalance of the centres identified that Fours can get caught in a feeling–thinking interactive loop. Breaking the loop requires them to connect into the body centre. Staying connected into the body centre is a method for preventing the interactive loop from recurring. When this is achieved, Fours can fully access the thinking centre and all of its gifts through conscious practices.

Physical activity provides this connection by grounding the Four. A brisk walk or other simple physical activity is a good way to achieve this. If you work in an office, climb the stairs rather than using the lift to go to meetings. When you are grounded, notice the impact on the clarity of your thinking.

Another approach is to listen to upbeat music that is energising and gets the body moving. Energetic dancing is a great way of connecting into the body, as is singing a favourite song. Notice what it feels like when you are connected into your body and look at how to re-create this feeling on a daily basis. What practices can you use to re-create this?

Balanced breathing is a quick way to balance the autonomic nervous system (responsible for control of the bodily functions not consciously directed, such as breathing, the heartbeat and digestive processes). It will also help you to connect your three centres together. Balanced breathing is achieved by taking a slow six-second breath in followed by a six-second breath out, repeating this for at least three minutes. Six or nine minutes will increase the effectiveness and give better results.

With the doing centre now connected, Fours now find it easy to access the undistorted clarity of the thinking centre.

Good self-care is also essential. Ensure that you have beneficial sleep and nutrition and regular exercise. Enjoy the creative side of cooking and the gourmet delicacies you can generate.

Having a clear intent as a type 4

In creating the habit of having a clear intent, the following are some suggested words that can strengthen emotional health for the Four: genuine, unique, appreciating, self-revealing, artistic, sensitive.

Type 5 somatic development guide

Connecting into their body centre is a key to a Five's development. The imbalance of the centres identified that Fives can get caught in a thinking–feeling interactive loop. Breaking the loop requires them to connect into the body centre. Staying connected into the body centre is also a method for preventing the interactive loop from recurring. When this is achieved, Fives can fully access the feeling centre and all of its gifts through conscious practices.

Balanced breathing is a quick way to balance the autonomic nervous system (responsible for control of the bodily functions not consciously directed, such as breathing, the heartbeat and digestive processes). It will also help you to connect your three centres together. Balanced breathing is achieved by taking a slow six-second breath in followed by a six-second breath out, repeating this for at least three minutes. Six or nine minutes will increase the effectiveness and give better results.

Physical activity provides connection to the body centre through the Five becoming grounded. Going for a brisk walk of at least twenty minutes will start to make this happen. Climbing flights of stairs rather than using the lift is another good way to do this, as are cycling, gym workouts, aerobic exercise and even singing. Notice the impact on you when you do these activities. Moving to action creates more energy for action.

Something else you can do is listen to upbeat music that energises you and gets you moving. Energetic dancing is a great way of connecting into the body, as is singing your favourite song. Notice what it feels like when you are connected into your body and look at how to recreate this feeling on a daily basis. What practices can you use to re-create this?

With the doing centre now connected, Fives now find it easy to access the undistorted passion of the feeling centre.

Good self-care is essential for everyone. Ensure you have beneficial sleep and nutrition and maintain regular exercise.

Having a clear intent as a type 5

In creating the habit of having a clear intent, the following are some suggested words that can strengthen emotional health for the Five: perceptive, ingenious, curious, insightful, inventive, exploratory.

Type 6 somatic development guide

Connecting into their head centre is a key to a Six's development. The imbalance of the centres identified that Sixes can get caught in either a feeling–doing or a doing–feeling interactive loop, while segregating from their primary 'head' centre. Ironically, breaking either of the loops requires them to connect into the head centre. Staying connected into the head centre is a method for preventing the interactive loops from recurring. When this is achieved, Sixes can fully access the feeling or doing centre and all of its gifts through conscious practices.

Balanced breathing is a quick way to balance the autonomic nervous system (responsible for control of the bodily functions not consciously directed, such as breathing, the heartbeat and digestive processes). It will also help you to connect your three centres together. Balanced breathing is achieved by taking a slow six-second breath in followed by a six-second breath out, repeating this for at least three minutes. Six or nine minutes will increase the effectiveness and give better results.

Walking outside in nature helps the Six clear their mind and gives them clarity in their thinking. Sometimes just standing up and getting a glass of water or walking to the fridge can create the necessary moment of clarity.

Connecting into the head centre can sometimes be as simple as holding or resting your head in your hands, or simply putting your hands on your head. It is good to take notice of whether you already do this, or something similar, unconsciously. Try to bring these practices into your conscious thought.

Reflect on a time when your thinking was clear and concise. What were you doing when that occurred or just prior to it? How could you re-create this? It is good to use past practices to help us by recalling them and repeating them.

With the thinking centre now connected, Sixes find it easy to access the undistorted drive of the doing centre and/or the passion of the feeling centre.

Good self-care is essential for everyone. Ensure you have beneficial sleep and nutrition and maintain regular exercise.

Having a clear intent as a type 6

In creating the habit of having a clear intent, the following are some suggested words that can strengthen emotional health for the Six: alert, self-reliant, mutually accountable, persevering, troubleshooter, cooperative.

Type 7 somatic development guide

Connecting into the heart is a key to a Seven's development. The imbalance of the centres identified that Sevens can get caught in a thinking–doing interactive loop and that breaking that loop requires them to connect into the heart centre. Staying connected into the heart centre is a method for preventing the interactive loop from recurring. When this is achieved, Sevens can fully access the doing centre and all of its gifts through conscious practices.

As a first step, take a moment to connect with something or someone you love and *feel* that connection. Notice what you are feeling and allow this to permeate your whole body. Often placing an open hand over the heart speeds up this connection. Many people do this naturally in their communications so it is a very acceptable thing to do. Stay connected to this feeling and to your heart and notice the impact this has on how you now perceive what is going on around you. Stay connected to this feeling and your heart and also notice the impact this has on how you now perceive what is going on around you.

Balanced breathing is a quick way to balance the autonomic nervous system (responsible for control of the bodily functions not consciously directed, such as breathing, the heartbeat and digestive processes). It will also help you to connect your three centres together. Balanced breathing is achieved by taking a slow six-second breath in followed by a six-second breath out, repeating this for at least three minutes. Six or nine minutes will increase the effectiveness and give better results.

Listen to music of the heart and fully connect with your heart into the love and passion of the music and the words. Dancing with intimacy can also connect you into your heart, especially if you fully immerse yourself in the feeling and experience. Dancing with structure and coordination with others also works.

Try gentle walking to quiet the mind as a lead-up to a sitting meditation that includes connecting into your heart. Practise connecting into your heart quickly, so that this becomes something you can recall as needed.

With the feeling centre connected, Sevens now find it easy to access the undistorted drive of the doing centre.

Good self-care is essential for everyone. Ensure you have beneficial sleep and nutrition and maintain regular exercise.

Having a clear intent as a type 7

In creating the habit of having a clear intent, the following are some suggested words that can strengthen emotional health for the Seven: joyful, enthusiastic, uplifting, accomplished, versatile, synthesizing.

Final words

One of our early teachers Robert Flynn encouraged us to always continue to explore our understanding of ourselves. Of the application of the Enneagram, he would often challenge us by saying, 'If that is not true for you, then what is?'

As we continue on own our journeys towards more self-awareness, towards a greater understanding of our own behaviours and impact, towards more time being 'present', we hope you will join us. We trust you have enjoyed this book and found it informative, and that it will help and inspire you to continue on your journey of self-development and a higher level of emotional health.

Beyond that, we encourage you to look at ways you can help improve the level of emotional health in others around you and in the organisations you work in and with, and therefore the impact they are having.

What can you do to make the world a more emotionally health place?

References and further reading

We first came across the terms 'horizontal' and 'vertical' in reference to leadership development in the work of the Center for Creative Leadership (www.ccl.org)

For more on what modern neuroscience has to say about the body, heart and head see the work of Grant Soosalu and Marvin Oka in their book *mBraining – Using your multiple brains to do cool stuff* and at www.mbraining.com, and that of Antonio Dimasio at www.antoniodamasio.com.

Our emotional health levels are adapted from pioneering work on the Enneagram by Don Riso and Russ Hudson and what they call the nine 'levels of development'. See www.enneagraminstitute.com

Our book *The Emotionally Healthy Leader* offers the opportunity to meet three 'emotionally healthy' leaders and understand what they do to build and strengthen their own emotional health. It also provides very practical suggestions as to how we can all move up the emotional health levels through conscious choices and mindful practices.

For more information on the impact of the instinctual variants on the Enneagram types and the creation of 27 subtypes, see *The Complete Enneagram: 27 Paths to Greater Self-Awareness* by Beatrice Chestnut.

Other books we often refer to include:

- *The Wisdom of the Enneagram* by Don Riso and Russ Hudson

- *Understanding the Enneagram* by Don Riso and Russ Hudson

- *The Essential Enneagram* by David Daniels and Virginia Price

- *The Enneagram Development Guide* by Ginger Lapid Bogda

- *The Art of Typing* by Ginger Lapid Bogda

- *The Complete Enneagram* by Bea Chestnut

- *The Enneagram* by Richard Rohr and Andrea Ebert

- *The Enneagram* in Love and Work by Helen Palmer

- *Knowing Me Knowing Them: Understanding your parenting personality by discovering the Enneagram* by Tracy Tresidder, Margaret Loftus and Jacqui Pollock

- *The Spiritual Dimension of the Enneagram* by Sandra Maitri.

About the authors

As the co-founders of Global Leadership Foundation, Malcolm Lazenby and Gayle Hardie are passionate about making a positive difference to people's lives, their businesses and communities – both local and global.

Along with their enthusiasm, Malcolm and Gayle bring over 35 years of experience and recognised expertise in: leadership development and transformation; emotional health and leadership resilience; strategic planning and implementation; organisation and cultural transformation; and board and executive mentoring and coaching.

Malcolm and Gayle's work on the emotional health levels of leaders and their 'translation' of the Enneagram (the study of nine basic personality types and their interrelationship) into practical and tangible business applications are recognised across the globe as both innovative and groundbreaking.

Malcolm has a Bachelor of Education and a Graduate Diploma in Human Resource Management. His skills were strengthened through senior leadership and management roles in the service sector and significant consulting experience in leadership development, organisational transformation and emotional intelligence.

Malcolm's work in the application and measurement of Emotional Intelligence within an Australian business environment is recognised as leading edge and he continues to be approached by researchers (particularly from the USA) to use his evaluation methodology.

Gayle has a Bachelor of Science in Human Relations and Organisational Behaviour and a Master of Arts (minor in Psychology). She has held significant roles in both the public and private sectors focusing on organisation development and change and strengthening community leadership.

Among other achievements, Gayle is a Fellow and former board member of Leadership Victoria and is a recipient of the Business and Professional Women's Community Leadership Award.

Profit for a purpose

Global Leadership Foundation leads by example in its stewardship role, supporting a number of community programmes and not-for-profit organisations as volunteers, facilitators, mentors and philanthropists.

Global Leadership Foundation has also partnered with the Australian Communities Foundation to establish a tax-deductible fund for the development of leaders in communities. The profits of Global Leadership Foundation's corporate work are added to this fund on an annual basis.

Global Leadership Profile

If you are interested in continuing your ongoing development, increasing your self-awareness and realising the impact of your emotional health levels and Enneagram types on yourself and others, you may be interested in the Global Leadership Profile.

The Global Leadership Profile is a vertical development tool, helping you to understand the way in which you lead and engage others and the impact you have on them. Drawing on many of the concepts described in this book, it provides insight into what drives and motivates you, how you react in certain situations, and why you may be 'stuck' in some of your practices. It then supports you in understanding the implications of what is revealed, with your results easily interpreted using this book as a guide.

The Profile is a 360° assessment and feedback process conducted entirely via secure online surveys.

For more information about the Global Leadership Profile, visit
www.globalleadershipfoundation.com/leadershipprofile
or contact us at leaders@globalleadershipfoundation.com

Global Leadership Foundation Enneagram cards

There are many tools for discovering more about who you are, what you prefer and how you engage with others and the world around you. The Global Leadership Foundation Enneagram cards provide you with the opportunity to explore each of the nine personality types in more detail. They describe each type's preferred ways of behaving and engaging at different emotional health levels. The cards use the same descriptors found in each of the emotional health continuums described in this book. They offer you another way of discovering what is 'most like you' as you begin your journey of self-discovery.

The Global Leadership Foundation Enneagram cards can be purchased from our online store at:

www.globalleadershipfoundation.com/store

Also available are a sorting map and instruction booklet. If you are new to the Enneagram, we highly recommend you purchase the complete set that includes an instruction book for using the cards.

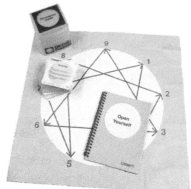

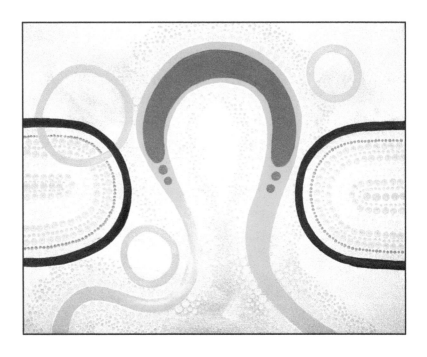

About the cover

'You are'

Acrylic on canvas 60x40cm
By Patrice Muthaymiles Mahoney, 2019

As we move along the many pathways throughout our lives, we come across challenges in   all aspects of our lives, not just professional spaces.

This painting was made with the thoughts of how, why and where we lead in our lives and what that looks like. The serene blue moving line represents the life each of us is moving with. The motion of living our journey with fulfilment can be solid and confident, hard and translucent, and wide with many challenges.

The dots surrounding the journey of life are all the decisions we make to stay on our path.

The blue-grey circular marks are the supports you have in life: mentors, family, partners or spirituality to help you on your journey. Your narrative is your story – no-one else can understand all the challenges you have on your journey, your life of leadership.

The circular dots inside these lines are the supports behind your supports. We often forget that we are from our parents, our parent's parents and so on for thousands of years. Our ancestral past has helped us be where we are today and our supporters have thousands of years of ancestors who've helped them all be where they are today.

The yellow circles are the stages we experience, grow and move through during our lives, in and out of loneliness, intention or participation.

All these elements, choices and intent together make this piece of work's elements relate together to create a narrative of leadership.

Living the life you want with intention and joy is the powerful leadership we are all seeking in ourselves.

reprint: 1.4/01-21

CPSIA information can be obtained
at www.ICGtesting.com
Printed in the USA
BVHW091332030522
635995BV00049B/2387